About the Author

Henk Carpentier Alting was born in Amsterdam, speaks Dutch, and spent his early childhood in Hong Kong.

His education continued in the UK, leading to a BSc in aeronautical engineering and an MSc in numerical analysis. A career in computing and management followed in the Aerospace industry. After redundancy, he joined a management training consultancy. Finally, chemotherapy gave him the unexpected opportunity to change direction and return to academic studies later in life at Manchester University.

Henk had an ongoing interest in philosophy. An MPhil in the Philosophy of Religion was followed by a PhD with the later thought of Ludwig Wittgenstein in the background. This developed his interest in language. While Wittgenstein is not the subject of this book beyond some examples, his influence is present.

A greater influence was that of John Walton, who opened Henk's eyes to the understanding of the ancient Near East in which the Genesis creation account is located. Within that ancient background, the significance of giving a name was the entry to this book's theme: the creative power of human language. With this theme, Henk develops not only a scriptural understanding of language, but also emphasises the dignity of humanity and our being in the image of God.

Henk is married to Sue, lives in Manchester, enjoys playing the piano and is active in his local church. He served for many years on his Diocesan Synod and is a volunteer with a hospital chaplaincy service.

Dedication

This book is dedicated to Professor John Walton, who opened my eyes to the implications of the Genesis creation account arising within the wider culture of the ancient Near East. Not only is that ancient world a fascinating subject, without a proper cultural context this book could not have been written.

Henk Carpentier Alting

THE CREATIVE WORD

AUSTIN MACAULEY PUBLISHERS®
LONDON * CAMBRIDGE * NEW YORK * SHARJAH

Copyright © Henk Carpentier Alting 2025

The right of Henk Carpentier Alting to be identified as author of this work has been asserted by the author in accordance with sections 77 and 78 of the Copyright, Designs and Patents Act 1988.

All rights reserved. No part of this publication may be reproduced, stored in a retrieval system, or transmitted in any form or by any means, electronic, mechanical, photocopying, recording, or otherwise, without the prior permission of the publishers.

Any person who commits any unauthorised act in relation to this publication may be liable to criminal prosecution and civil claims for damages.

A CIP catalogue record for this title is available from the British Library.

ISBN 9781035857630 (Paperback)
ISBN 9781035857647 (ePub e-book)

www.austinmacauley.com

First Published 2025
Austin Macauley Publishers Ltd®
1 Canada Square
Canary Wharf
London
E14 5AA

Acknowledgements

I would like to thank Austin Macauley for taking on a first-time author and providing all the assistance and background work that goes into publishing a book.

I would also thank those friends who have made comments from time to time. Their feedback was extremely helpful in improving the overall clarity of my writing. Of course, any shortcomings remain my own.

Most of all I thank my wife, Sue, for her support, particularly when I should have been doing other things instead of writing this book.

Table of Contents

Preface

There is a saying which goes: "Sticks and stones may break my bones but words will never hurt me." No doubt this expresses noble sentiments of resilience and perhaps even humility. However, words and even single-word names can do immense damage to a person's reputation.

There is a creative power in human language—for good or evil, truth or falsehood, clarity or obfuscation. Such linguistic creativity and its origin are the theme of this book.

What drew me to the topic of language and its creative ability?

I was a latecomer to the subject and at that point still some way from a scriptural perspective on language. My interest in language was initially stimulated by Ludwig Wittgenstein who was in the background of my PhD.

That scriptural perspective became much clearer on coming across the work of John Walton. My previous vague and ill-informed views on the context of the ancient Near East (ANE) and its bearing on the Genesis creation account received a new direction. It was through the ancient significance of a name being part of a thing's existence that I saw a way into my theme on the creative power of language.

The setting of the Genesis creation account in the wider cultural context of the ANE is not a subject in which I have any expertise. I will rely on Walton's work and to a lesser extent on John Hilber to deal with background issues for my theme. These two scholars present a slightly contrasting emphasis which I take to be complementary. I will say a little more about their approach since it was so helpful to me in developing my theme.

Walton shows the ancient focus on creation's order and its 'function' in the sense of progressing a goal-directed purpose to bring order from an initial non-order. The maintenance of the resulting order was a major concern of the ANE.

While there was an understanding of the material aspect of creation affecting everyday life, that was not a significant concern of the creation accounts. This very likely applies to the Genesis creation account as well as the surrounding creation stories, though the roles, character and being of the neighbouring gods were very different from the God of the Hebrews.

Hilber has a somewhat different emphasis as he describes various ways by which material considerations were never far from their conceptual world, including the origin stories. For believers with a high view of Scripture, that raises the unsettling possibility of Scripture being mistaken in matters relating to material structures, given our current scientific knowledge.

Hilber addresses this by applying a linguistic approach where God accommodates our human understanding, which has similarities to what we ourselves do in our everyday speaking. I found this not only helpful, but also an important means to progress my linguistic theme.

With the work of Walton and Hilber, I felt I could develop a perspective on human language which does justice to the Genesis account and the limited ancient understanding of material causes, processes and structures. It also enabled me to see human language as being creative in a way which mirrors the creative speaking of God.

These comments lead naturally to the book's title, *The Creative Word*. I might even summarise this by the question: What is the significance of Adam naming those animals?

It is inevitable that my academic studies influenced my approach, at least to some extent. For example, I do not propose to rely much on philosophical or theological arguments and theories. Instead, I will use examples of language use to develop my theme, which also helps to see how that ancient understanding relates to our own in different ways. This descriptive rather than theorising approach is typical of Wittgenstein's later philosophy. However, apart from a few of his examples along with an occasional explanatory note, I take his thought no further; my interests lie elsewhere.

This book is not intended for those who might want more in-depth material on the ANE, philosophy, theology, biblical studies or the Hebrew text of Genesis. Particularly with the ANE and the biblical text, I have relied on the knowledge of experts.

This book is intended for those who take an intelligent interest in their faith by looking at the 'big picture' rather than all the fine detail. If readers' interests are stimulated to look further into particular areas, the relevant references are in the text and notes. In the case of the ANE, I would certainly recommend readers do so if the subject is unfamiliar to them. I found that ANE background particularly helpful and indeed, a fascinating topic in its own right.

While the ANE background is an important contextual aspect of the Genesis creation account, I also need to show its relevance to contemporary readers. I try to do this with illustrations from our own language and practices.

One aspect of relevance is that our linguistic creativity takes place within a complex mix of social and personal factors, including controversial cultural trends. While I have had a marginal church involvement in watching these trends develop, I will not analyse them in detail, which many writers have done better than I could. However, such contemporary trends provide excellent illustrations which I will use on occasions alongside many others.

To conclude, readers may not agree with all the material which builds my theme. However, I hope that I have conveyed something of the relevance of the Genesis creation account for our lives today. And in particular, something of our dignity as human beings made in the image of God. Despite so much evil and tragedy along the way, I believe that dignity will nevertheless be finally established through Jesus Christ.

Anticipating just some of the coming material in this book, it is Christ who opens the door for us to receive a new name and abide with God in a temple as it were, a new creation which embraces heaven and earth. (Rev 3:12)

In this, the last book of Bible echoes that Genesis creation account, with naming and temple terms which were probably better understood by those ancient Hebrews than they are by many of us.

I hope my book helps us to better understand the relevance of that ancient Genesis narrative.

1. Introduction

What's in a name?
That which we call a rose by any other word would smell as sweet.
William Shakespeare: Romeo and Juliet[1]

In Act 2, Scene 2, Juliet says the above to Romeo. How can the family names of the Montagues and Capulets, their family names, incorporate an enmity that threatens their love? Surely a mere name cannot have that power. The love between Romeo and Juliet transcends those names, or any other words for that matter.

Just as a rose's sweet smell is unaffected by whatever that flower's name might be, so her love for that same person, Romeo, endures whatever Romeo's family name might be. The real person, Romeo, surely lives beyond an arbitrary and ephemeral name.

"What's in a name?"

Nevertheless, while only a name, it is that family name which Juliet finds so hostile, even though she denies it. "'Tis but thy name which is my enemy, Thou art thyself." Their family names are experienced as almost *being* inter-family enmity because those names are embedded in that lived enmity.

Similarly, the name 'rose' may be much more than a changeable label for a flower. The name itself conveys something of the reality of that beautiful flower and its sweet smell, which we experience with so much pleasure in our lives.

There may be a great deal to those names, and to many other kinds of names we assign. Names often embody a deeper context of lived human reality than merely being a convenient and changeable label for reference purposes. Juliet uses the rose-named metaphor to good effect, though it also undermines itself.

---

[1] Shakespeare (no date), from the online Folger Shakespeare Library.

Even more compelling are their own names, 'Romeo and Juliet', which echo down the centuries with an enduring significance for us today.[2]

1.1 Thematic Outline

To name something is at the heart of this book. While Juliet questioned the significance of a name, at the start of the Bible we find Adam naming the animals. And before that, God also names the parts of creation. When we then find God not only naming, but that his speaking brings creation into being, human language may have a creative power of its own. In a nutshell, that is the theme of this book.

Language is an enormously complex and varied subject, so we have to narrow our focus or point of view, which we might call selecting a 'perspective'. That perspective may also come with unmentioned assumptions, which we should bring to light.

We are not concerned with details like spelling, grammar, parts of speech, punctuation, expressing ourselves clearly and all the useful things, which, hopefully, we learnt from our parents and at school. Neither are we concerned with the historical development of different languages, relations between them, the many forms and genres of literature, the endlessly varied ways of speaking and rhetorical techniques, or the theories of linguists.

Our major focus is on the significance of language within the wider purpose of human life as seen from the perspective of the Christian faith. Hence, the Genesis creation account is also at the heart of this book.

However, in coming to the Genesis creation, we must begin with some preparatory work. The last thing we should think about is modern science. Rather, we will try to enter the cultural context of the ancient Near East (ANE) from which Genesis originates.

Other cultures[3] may look at the world in a rather different way to our own, though these might also be related since we live in the same world. I was once told that "to get into someone else's shoes, we must first step out of our own shoes."

---

[2] More detail about the metaphorical aspects of Juliet's rose is in section 5.1.

[3] The term 'culture' does not refer to a particular society but to a society's practices and beliefs.

This shows the two-sided nature of the task. To see things from another culture's perspective, we must first recognise our own often unquestioned assumptions. Leaving those behind is to get out of our own shoes.

Hopefully, none of this contextual emphasis will be news to any student of literature, or of the Bible.

Hence, two preparatory chapters follow this introduction. We first look in more detail at the ANE context to identify common elements with Genesis as well as significant contrasts. A particularly important matter is the significance of a name in the ANE, which for them was necessary for something to fully exist.

We will also see that the Genesis creation account and the ANE were much less concerned with material causes, processes and structures than we are. Their interest was with the role different elements played within the whole and in relation to the gods, or to the God of the Hebrews.

Put differently, the ANE was concerned with order and function as in role or purpose, rather than material properties, causes and structures. The fear of our world falling into disorder or non-order was a real one. Those cultural differences make it hard for us to enter into that ancient world of thought.

However, there are common elements which we will consider, particularly in the second preparatory chapter. We are not entirely disconnected from those ancient people since we all live in God's ordered creation.

Following this preparatory work, we come to Adam naming the animals. This is not a moment for hilarity; him naming the animals is reflected in so many of our own practices. We then relate our speaking to the image of God in ourselves and our mandate to populate the world and rule it as good stewards or vice-regents on God's behalf.

This implies we investigate and come to understand more of His creation, which Adam starts to do in naming the animals. Such an understanding is coupled with our language having a creative aspect, which mirrors in a derivative way God's creative word in the Genesis creation account. At this point, we have reached the heart of a scriptural perspective on human language.

We then proceed with examples to show something of the wider creative ability of our language, and how it is *creative*. By now, the reader will likely have potential objections, which we must deal with. The most serious is where Genesis portrays some aspects of the creation in a way which we now know to be mistaken, arising from that same linguistic creativity. We must consider how to deal with this without losing the authority and reliability of scripture.

To finish, we consolidate our theme with two important topics.

The first is that God sees His creative work as 'good', indeed it was 'very good'. We will relate this to our own speaking of what is 'good', and see how value, purpose and significance is integrated into creation. We also take account of eating the fruit from that tree of the knowledge of good and evil in the garden, which is the tree of wisdom.

This has consequences for our linguistic creativity—for good or evil.

Then secondly, how do we speak about and to God, which we have largely taken for granted so far? God is a being who is not of this world and is beyond our comprehension, yet we cannot avoid using the language of our familiar life. Our linguistic creativity will need some contextual constraint if it is not to distort our understanding of the being of God.

The conclusion at the end will consolidate our material, and particularly the relevance of the creative power of our language shown in contemporary cultural trends.

This brief overview of our direction of travel may seem a little abstract, so there will be numerous examples to help us along.

To make a final introductory comment on the scope of this book, I am not overly concerned with the detailed exegesis of the Genesis text or what might be the precise meaning of Hebrew terms. When necessary, I shall reference the expertise of others.

The wider cultural background of the ANE is itself a large subject. For readers who wish to look at this in depth, I shall reference a few important works. For my purpose, I will confine myself to what is necessary to progress my theme.

Two other disciplines have a bearing on this book's theme. These are philosophy and theology, which have both developed significantly over many centuries. Like the sciences, they may also become the lens through which we see the ANE context and may thereby distort it.

However, there are a few useful philosophical terms and related concepts for us to be familiar with, so some introductory comments on these two disciplines are called for.

1.2 A Philosophical Perspective - Two Important Terms

To start with philosophy, there has always been an interest in language where the philosophy of language is an extensive subject. However, it has traditionally been rather a poor relation among other philosophical topics.[4] The most prominent philosophical concerns have been around what it means for something to exist as one thing rather than another (ontology), knowledge (epistemology), logic, ethics and aesthetics. The term 'ontology' has a place in this book and in the literature to which I refer, so I should say a little more about it.

We need to distinguish different kinds of *being*, as Adam does in naming the animals. What these kinds of being *are* is an *ontological* question. For example, a human being is at least in part a material being, and in that respect has a material ontology along with other material objects.

By contrast, though numbers are applied to material objects in counting for example, a number itself is not a material object, so can be considered as having a non-material or abstract ontology. Many philosophers have searched for some fundamental or essential ontological characteristic which separates different categories of being. This may then lead to a definition of what something *is*.

However, we can also consider a human being from different ontological aspects, or complementary ways of what we *are*. There is a material ontological aspect along with the aspect of being in the image of God, which is not a material ontological category.

If we ask what is most fundamental about human beings, a Christian believer will most likely say it is the image of God, since that uniquely distinguishes us from all other material animals and living systems. Differing ontological perspectives are important as we continue.

Another common philosophical term is 'metaphysics', which concerns the fundamental nature of reality. The basic idea is how the experience of our senses or our thinking and reasoning relate to that which in some way lies outside of, or is other than ourselves and our faculties.

We might say that our mind and concepts mirror or map onto a 'reality', which is other than our mind and concepts. Hence, metaphysical questions frequently underlie other topics, including ontology.

Again to briefly illustrate, we might say the existence of God or some foundation to ethics are what we believe or feel within ourselves as true about

---

[4] Rush Rhees was a student, friend and writer on Ludwig Wittgenstein's philosophy. Rhees notes that Bertrand Russell thought there were more important questions than a philosophical concern with language. (Rhees 2004, 1) Neither Wittgenstein nor Rhees would have shared Russell's view.

what is beyond or transcends ourselves. To call these 'metaphysical questions' indicates something of the philosophical character of our reference to the being of God or a foundation to ethics.

Then, if language, mind and that external reality can be related by a more detailed metaphysical model or theory, we might be more confident about having access to true knowledge of such an external reality.[5]

If we now approach our language theme from a metaphysical perspective, whatever else it does, a name *refers* to something. Terms such as 'human person', 'image of God', the number 'one' or a material object such as a 'brain' distinguished from a 'mind', are all names which refer to different ontological categories or kinds.

If we then consider *how* the name refers to those ontologically different kinds of existents, we have an example of a metaphysical question. We are trying to move from human language to a reality which we refer to but lies outside our language, reason and what we perceive through our senses.[6]

Such an approach would traditionally be considered the philosophical task in dealing with a metaphysical question. If metaphysics sounds an abstruse subject remote from everyday life, indeed it is. This detachment from everyday life is shown when philosophers question the casual use of the term 'real' or 'reality' as in "What do you mean by 'real'?"

This is due to a potential metaphysical gap between our sense perceptions, thinking, concepts and even language itself, distinguished from what's 'really out there'. Readers might be relieved that we will not deal with the many and varied metaphysical theories about reality.

However, there will be occasions when we need to move from our speaking to what our speaking is about, which is particularly so with God. When we do

---

[5] Ontological and metaphysical questions go back at least as far as Aristotle. He did not coin the term 'metaphysics' but called this investigation 'first philosophy'. (Aristotle 1998, 155, Epsilon: 1) Aristotle was concerned with the branch of metaphysics we would now call ontology, the nature or being and existence of what there is. A closely related question is in what sense differing ontologies can be said to *exist*.

[6] A metaphysical investigation of the nature of reality also goes beyond scientific inquiry. Specific metaphysical topics include the nature of existence, causation, necessity, mind and its relation to matter, consciousness, space and time, determinism and free-will, change and permanence.

so, we will use varied examples as illustrations to assist us with what, from a philosophical perspective, is a metaphysical question.

The reader, particularly those with little philosophical background, might note in passing how these new philosophical terms, or *names* of concepts rather than objects, help us see our relation to the world in different ways. It is an early example of the creative power of language, which is our theme.

I will not focus on philosophical issues and mostly confine any philosophical and more academic details to the supplementary numbered notes. However, I admit that the various philosophical systems we now have were produced by some of the greatest minds in response to questions that continually fascinate us. Indeed, many have touched on important aspects of created realities. Even so, the complex subtlety of creation seems to have defied all-embracing philosophical theories.

Philosophical discussions have a serious purpose, often trying to get to the truth. They should not be lightly dismissed. We should also recognise that some outstanding philosophers have taken a more sceptical approach to philosophy, particularly to metaphysical theorising. Yet there have been helpful developments in the philosophy of language, some of which influences this book.

So, we should say something more positive about philosophy which finds a place in this book. Philosophers are rarely experts in the technical details of a subject that is their interest. For example, philosophers of science might not make any significant contribution to scientific knowledge. What they do is probe and question matters which influence but also lie outside the body of scientific knowledge.

They might investigate how the predominant beliefs in a society influenced scientific developments. They might ask on what basis we supposedly 'know' the principle of the uniformity of nature or why the natural world has a striking mathematical character.[7]

---

[7] For example, R. Hooykaas contrasts Greek with Christian and biblical thought, when the latter became less dependent on Greek philosophy. The world being much like and organism was replaced by a mechanism in the scientific developments of the sixteenth century. (Hooykaas 1973, 13). For the world as organism see Plato 1977, §30–31, §42–43. While the Christian faith had a significant influence on scientific developments, it was also a complex and sometimes fraught relation. (Spencer 2016, 94–109) Details are in Gaukroger 2008, see for example Gaukroger, 455 ff.

These questions certainly require reasonable knowledge of relevant scientific developments. However, it will not include holding a test tube in a laboratory while wearing a white coat and submitting the results to a learned journal, to make the point a little crudely.

This book does something similar by avoiding technical linguistic details while asking questions about the bigger picture of language in human life, creation and in relation to God Himself.

Doubtless, my outline so far on some of the philosophical aspects of our subject needs a much fuller treatment. While we will occasionally touch on philosophical and metaphysical issues, we need to go elsewhere to achieve a credible perspective on language.

I turn next to the theology of the Christian faith.

1.3 A Theological and Scriptural Perspective

To close this introduction, I make two further qualifications on the theological perspective, in addition to the thematic outline presented earlier. (1.1)

Firstly, I will place myself within the Christian faith and its roots in the Bible. That is the faith I know. For me to refer to other religions may lead to their distortion. My focus on the Christian faith is also part of my own commitment, which includes what might be called a more traditional or high view of the authority of scripture.

I should disclose my own beliefs since these inevitably influence my approach to the subject. The same might be said for any other approach; a wholly neutral or supposedly objective vantage point is not possible. Yet, I hope I can be self-critical when required, and aware not just of my own limits but also of the influence of our contemporary Western culture on myself; it is hard to eliminate that completely.

Secondly, when mentioning the creation account in Genesis 1–3, many believers will likely ask how my theme relates to the historicity of the account, including that of Adam and Eve. By 'historicity', I do not mean how and when Genesis originated and what different documents and traditions might be identified in the text we now have. I leave that to scholars in the relevant disciplines.[8]

---

[8] A brief overview of the changing character of debates on this point is in Walton 2018, 3–5. Confessional polemics were part of these debates. (Ibid. 26–30)

A different concern with historicity is whether the Genesis creation account deals with the age of the universe, whether the creation was brought into existence in six days similar to our own familiar days, the place of biological evolution and whether Adam and Eve as real people were created 'de novo', directly by God outside any evolutionary process or other material causes.

Such questions can dominate discussion about Genesis in some churches.

To go a little further, these questions are often framed in terms of the text having a 'literal' sense in contrast to a more metaphorical or perhaps poetic sense. The term 'literal' can be confusing. It usually means that words or concepts have a sense arising from our familiar life, with 'days' being 24-hour periods for example. There is no metaphor or other figurative language involved.

However, any 'literal' sense in an ancient culture may be very different to our own. That culture might not privilege familiar life or the material world as we do, affecting how we should apply any sense of 'literal' to them.

Another possible confusion is with the term 'creationist', which is sometimes used to characterise arguments for a young earth. Yet, surely all Christian believers accept that God created this universe and ourselves. All believers are in that sense 'creationists' while taking different positions on the historicity of the Genesis account.

In this book, I will not evaluate such questions given that our theme is human language. That theme requires us to position ourselves in the context of the ANE. This exposes us to a very different understanding of the world, which we will prioritise above philosophy, contemporary science and any wider cultural assumptions we hold.

Hence we must try to avoid reading contemporary debates into the text. Nevertheless, prioritising the ANE context has implications on debates about historicity in the sense above, if that context is not concerned with addressing the questions we pose.

Hopefully however, careful attention to the ancient context may give a more rewarding and faithful account of the Genesis creation, even if it leaves us with questions to which we do not have adequate answers. [9]

---

[9] Questions such as: why was there animal suffering and predation before human beings were present? Does Adam relate to a real human person in history, and if so, where does that fit into the development of the human race? If Adam was an archetype but not a real figure, how do we relate that to Romans 5:12–20? How does his disobedience relate to

We should remember what God said to Job: "Where were you when I laid the earth's foundation? Tell me if you understand. Who marked off its dimensions? Surely you know!" (Job 38: 4, 5) Job got no answers to such questions and so it may be for us, despite our scientific progress.

1.4 Chapter Outlines

The chapters which follow this introduction are briefly summarised below. They follow the thematic outline earlier (1.1).

2. The Context of the ancient Near East, opens with an important point, which continues throughout the book. Language is not confined to spoken words or written symbols following rules of grammar, though that is true as far as it goes. Our saying and doing are woven together within the lives we live. Furthermore, the lives we live are within a wider society, and hence the cultural context is important in understanding the Genesis text.

That leads to the chapter's main theme, which is to approach our subject from the cultural context of the ANE. To do this effectively, we must recognise and leave behind our own cultural background and embedded assumptions. Our focus is on the way the ANE thought about the 'existence' of something, and the importance of a 'name' being given.

Giving a name is also the entry to our theme of developing a perspective on language. The chapter closes by briefly comparing the Genesis creation account with the opening of the Babylonian creation epic, the *Enuma Elish,* to illustrate the position of Genesis within its wider cultural context. However, we will also note some very significant differences.

In this chapter, I will rely on specialist knowledge, particularly the work of John Walton, to set out the background on which I can then build.[10]

---

human beings before him who also suffered and died? Were such earlier creatures human at all, bearing the image of God? An overview of the interaction between theology, the Bible and science is in Madueme and Reeves, 2014. For an online overview of genetics and human genealogy in relation to theology see Hardin, 2019.

[10] John H. Walton (2018), *Ancient Near Eastern Thought and the Old Testament-Introducing the Conceptual World of the Hebrew Bible*. I also make use of other works of his.

3. Relating the Ancient to Our Contemporary World aims to show that while ANE thought and context are very different to our own, that ancient context is not entirely disconnected from our contemporary lives and practices.

In this chapter, we look at both similarities and differences to our own contemporary practices with some examples and analogies. That will help us leave our own assumptions behind while still having the continuity of a shared human life within God's creation.

4. The Creative Word: Adam Names the Animals moves to the heart of this book's theme. It draws together some brief and scattered points from the previous preparatory chapters by setting out the theme in four cumulative steps. The man, Adam, is our working example.

We first see him begin to understand the order of the world as he names the animals. We then relate his naming and understanding to the rule he is to exercise, being the image of God. We note the close relation between kings and the way their statues and other images were related to their patron deities. This has implications for the Genesis portrayal of the image of God in ourselves.

Then we go on to Adam naming the animals as mirroring the creative speaking or Word of God, which brings an ordered creation into being. Finally, we see how Adam's naming of the animals is itself in part a creative act, for which I introduce the term 'construct'.

5. Creativity and the Construct Model has more examples of our linguistic creativity, now employing a 'construct' approach. While Adam naming the animals remains in view, these examples go beyond the simple naming of objects. An important point is that the construct approach which I adopt does not float free from the realities of human life and God's ordered creation in which we are located.

It has been an ongoing theme that in our language the doing and saying are woven together into our lives and within God's creation. Hence, there are constraints on what we say, what makes sense, and that on many occasions our speaking and constructs can be critically verified—and need to be!

6. Some Objections and Challenges: Objections will occur to readers, and a few of the more serious ones are addressed in this chapter. Perhaps the most serious is the portrayal in Genesis of the structure of the cosmos.[11] While this is common enough in the ANE, it is hard to avoid concluding that it is mistaken.

How do we handle this if we want to maintain the authority of scripture? We also look at some challenges which are not so much objections to my theme but how we deal with the instability of contemporary linguistic constructs.

7. What is Creation's 'Good'? Here, we consider God viewing His creation as 'good'. What does that mean in the context of the ANE? Given our own varied use, how does the ANE relate to our use of the term? Most importantly, there is the tree of the knowledge of good and evil and how eating its fruit affects our linguistic constructs—for good or evil.

This chapter is to identify the varied sense of 'good'. It illustrates something of the creativity of our language, which is reflected in the Genesis account.

8. Speaking about and to God. Since God is other than this world, how do we use language which is rooted in human life within this created world when speaking about and to God the Creator? While there is a metaphorical element here, we must also make sense. We look at logical bounds to our speaking about God and how that logic of God is set within the context of scripture. We cannot conceptually construct God in our image!

9. Conclusion. Finally, we pull the major strands of the book together and apply them to some important trends in our Western culture. While somewhat more controversial, my purpose is to show that the Genesis creation account and its ancient context are still relevant for us today.

The emphasis is not on a critical or apologetic engagement with those trends, which has been well done by other writers, and is beyond the scope of this book. My purpose is to consolidate our theme of human linguistic creativity by showing again its remarkable creative and persuasive ability—for good or evil.

---

[11] 'Cosmos' is a frequently used term, for our purpose it is equivalent to 'creation'.

2. The Context of the Ancient Near East

We don't have to be a student of biblical studies to know the importance of context. To understand a written text and the language of a very different culture requires us to find out as much as we can about the wider cultural setting from which that text arose.

However, in some cases, an originating context may be elusive. For example, it might depend on the current state of archaeological excavations and the extent that ancient languages have been deciphered and translated. Little or even none of this may have been available until more recent times.

That is the case with the Genesis creation account and its location in the context of the ancient Near East (ANE), which is our theme in this chapter.

We should not conclude that understanding the Bible's message is compromised in the absence of surrounding historical and cultural detail. The thrust of a biblical passage is usually clear enough, particularly when supported elsewhere in the Bible.

However, improving our understanding of the cultural context enriches and deepens our faith, and it may on occasions correct us. This is similar to studying scholars and theologians from the past, or trying to improve the quality of the biblical text from the recovery and translation of ancient manuscripts. Recovering that cultural background requires work on our part; it does not come on a plate given us by God.

2.1 Preliminaries (i): Naming—Our Speaking and Doing Woven Together

As we look at how language conveys meaning within a wider cultural context, we readily focus on the big and important matters of societies and their practices and beliefs. We can then get down to the serious work of interpretation. While all that is important, we may lose sight of how a language is learnt from apparently trivial human practices starting in childhood.

Since God is the author of both the big issues and the trivia, we should not ignore the apparently trivial which anchors us in our surrounding society and culture from the very start of our lives. That childhood background also lays the ground for our own cultural assumptions, which is one factor making it difficult to enter the perspective of another culture.

So, let's start by asking how and why that initial learning is important. The focus here and in much of this chapter is on giving something a name, then going on to consider the scriptural significance of naming.

We often think of language as the spoken or written words and then ask how symbols as sounds or written marks are organised to convey meaning. But it is not merely speech or writing organised within rules of grammar that matter. All these are woven into our actions and hence into the practices of human life.

As a child learns a language, the use and meaning of words within developing speech are inseparable from their application in activity. It is through the saying and doing woven together that the child is also established in the life and beliefs of the surrounding society and its culture. Hence, the importance of context starts from our earliest years.

To take an example, in his *Confessions*, St Augustine reflects on a familiar linguistic practice, which may initially appear trivial but will be important as we continue. He relates how he learns the *names* of objects:

> "When they called some thing by name and pointed it out while they spoke, I saw it and realized that the thing they wished to indicate was called by the name they then uttered. And what they meant was made plain by the gestures of their bodies, by a kind of natural language, common to all nations, which expresses itself through changes of countenance, glances of the eye, gestures and intonations which indicate a disposition and attitude—either to seek or to possess, to reject or to avoid. So it was that by frequently hearing words, in different phrases, I gradually identified the objects which the words stood for and, having formed my mouth to repeat these signs, I was thereby able to express my will." [12]

[12] Augustine 1955, Book I, Chapter VIII, section 13.

According to St Augustine, learning the name of an object is part of a whole cluster of human *activity*, in this case what seems like trivial activity. While Augustine is born with in innate ability to learn a language, he does not have an innate grasp of what it is to name something, let's suppose it is a 'chair'.

He learns this in a context where the doing and saying are woven together. Along with the parental gestures which he describes, we should picture much more; he is made to sit still in the chair, move the chair, not spill his food on the chair and so forth.

He also learns to name other things such as his toys in the context of play; naming takes place across a variety of different contexts and activities. Augustine not only learns the names of things, but also *how* one names something. Finally, what those names mean is shown in how they are used both in the speaking and in the activities of the child's life.[13]

To illustrate this differently, suppose I say to someone who doesn't know what a chair is, "that's a chair." How do they know what I am referring to without pointing or some other context of engagement? And even if their attention is so directed, they still don't know what to make of the object unless this is explained or shown to them. They even have to understand the convention of pointing.

However, explanations are of limited value to a child who has not yet mastered a language, whereas engaging with the chair gives them a sense of what it is. The meaning of our speaking is inseparably connected with our doing, which starts from our earliest days.

Turning from concrete objects like a chair to more abstract concepts, that would also be in a context of activity. Perhaps Augustine learnt the names and the use of numbers by counting coins, adding some and taking some away, initially in play activity. And beyond that, he would of course have been learning social skills and taking on values.

Continuing with the chair, doubtless Augustine quickly mastered this simple practice of naming and using a name, along with appropriate gestures and

---

[13] The philosopher Ludwig Wittgenstein considers these questions by quoting the words from St Augustine at the start of his *Philosophical Investigations*. (Wittgenstein 1977, 2e, §1 ff.) Early in the *Investigations*, Wittgenstein mentions the doing and saying woven together as a 'language-game' (§7). The language-game metaphor indicates both rules such as grammar, and a freedom in playing the game within the rules. However, in order to make sense, words reside within the lives we live (§18); the saying should not be detached from the doing. These important points continue in the course of this book.

activity relating to the named objects. Then, over time, as he became a competent language user, the surrounding activity was increasingly taken for granted, used and interpreted without further thought.

Unsurprisingly, we then give it little further attention. However, Augustine gave it his attention and came to reflect on how he learnt the names of things.[14]

Learning a name will include activity which conveys value. Hence, learning value-words is similar to learning material object-words in that the sense of value is again conveyed through actions and social practices.

For example, the status of the mother and women more generally will be conveyed to a child in the context of family life. There may be slaves within the family in a slave-owning culture. Their value will be expressed by actions in family and community life. Some slaves may be valued but many others will be treated poorly. Even today, some cultures regard some human beings as untouchables, elsewhere girls are subject to brutal treatment.[15]

The relevance to our theme is that value-laden actions within language learning have a bearing on upholding or negating the image of God, just as much as learning the name of a chair. We are embedded in a culture across all aspects of our lives, for good or evil, since our spoken language, beliefs and understanding are woven together in activity and human life from the start.

That is why context of the ANE is so important if we are to understand the Genesis account more fully. What might Genesis share with the ANE, and importantly, what does it oppose? How do we relate to this? All of us are embedded in our surrounding culture from our earliest years.

If my women and slave illustration of value-language is unfamiliar, it illustrates why trying to understand another culture, particularly an ancient one,

---

[14] Wittgenstein is critical of Augustine who takes a name as referring to objects such as say, a 'chair', which is too limited a view of naming within wider language use. Wittgenstein rightly draws attention to the variety of naming practices to deal with numbers, colours, thoughts, motives, values and so on. However, Augustine points us to a wider context of *activity* or *practices* in which the names of objects are learned, which Wittgenstein would have agreed with. (Wittgenstein 1977, 2e, §1 ff)

[15] Nigel Biggar gives the example of female genital circumcision or mutilation (FGM). He describes how Christian missionaries campaigned against FGM among the Kikuyu in central Kenya. We note that FGM was an established cultural practice with social significance. (Biggar 2023, 85) What was said, believed and done were closely bound together and children would become aware of this socially important practice.

is no easy task. We constantly risk looking at others through the lens of what is familiar to ourselves, powerfully influenced by what we uncritically absorbed in childhood. The doing and saying together anchor us in our surrounding culture.

That contemporary culture and its assumptions are what we must try to set aside as we approach our theme, though at some point we must also exercise our critical faculties about a cultural background. We will do so in due course by looking at objections, but then the Genesis account does likewise in its opposition to some of the beliefs of the time, particularly about the deities.

2.2 Preliminaries (ii): Contemporary Assumptions and a Material Ontology

Having noted the importance of context, there is one further preliminary to deal with. We should be clear about the likely assumptions we ourselves hold since we are also part of a cultural context with its own understanding and perspectives.

That understanding starts in childhood as we saw with St Augustine, and it is ingrained in us. The danger is that our contemporary understanding will form the lens through which we view the Genesis text.

To be specific, the opening of Genesis is an account of creation and therefore deals with the *existence* of the many and varied constituent objects of that creation. But how do we, from our contemporary Western culture and its science-informed background, conceive of an object as 'existing'?

While we will not focus on philosophy and associated metaphysical theories, that does not mean we have nothing to say about the meaning of something to 'exist', particularly when considering a material object. Suppose someone says: "Certainly the spider-crab exists; it can grow more than twice the size of a human. I have seen one myself." How do we explain this everyday sense of the spider-crab *existing*?

We might say it is apparent to some or all the five senses as in the above, "I have *seen* one myself." This is just familiar speaking. But living in a society shaped by scientific developments, we may also highlight other aspects of existent objects, which we investigate by more subtle means than our five senses.

In the creation and the Genesis account, the earth and the heavenly bodies are prominent. With these, we not only think of physical objects like the stars and planets, but also about the causal processes and timescales to form them, and the details of the resulting material structures.

We use scientific terms or names like mass, force, gravity, velocity, distances measured in 'light years', hydrogen and other elements, 'black holes' and much more. The result is a complex but rewarding cosmology which is part of our scientific knowledge, specifically the physical sciences.[16]

Even if we are not trained scientists ourselves, a great deal of our thinking about the world is suffused with that scientific background; we scarcely give it a second thought. Put in philosophical terms, our contemporary perspective is dominated by a *material ontology*.

Generally speaking, things exist as material objects which are structured within a complex of causes and processes. I introduced the term 'ontology' earlier as referring to the existence or being of something. We do not always need philosophical theories about this and can use the term in a more general sense as we do here.[17]

We then read the Genesis creation account and are stopped in our tracks. Surely, we 'know', at least in reasonable outline, how the heavenly bodies, including the earth itself, developed through these causal processes over long periods of time.

Careful observation of the heavenly bodies again confirms the same physical laws and processes we encounter here on earth. What then are we to make of the Genesis account? How do we interpret the 'days' and the sequence in which the different parts of creation were brought to existence, just to start somewhere with

---

[16] 'Science' should not be understood as reference to a single monolithic activity of ours. There are many sciences with different though related methods. For example, when thinking about creation, the physical sciences such as physics and chemistry come to mind, closely related to cosmology and astronomy.

These physical sciences move into the biochemistry of living organisms with applications in medical practices. As drugs, physical substances are used to alleviate mental conditions by interacting with the physical structures of the brain. Sciences dealing with the mind and human behaviour such as psychology differ markedly from the physical sciences in their methods, while being inter-related. Additionally, there are the social sciences, again with their own focus and methods.

We should also note different ways we use the term 'exist'. For example, does a company exists when certain legal procedures are complete or when it has premises? We might prefer to say it exists when it starts doing business. (Walton 2009, 21–22) These different ways of speaking are important as we continue.

[17] I will follow Walton in the use of the term 'material ontology'. (Walton 2015a, 23)

our questions? And finally, we have the creation of living things, which came about through a process of evolution over long periods of time, surely.

To expand on what we noted briefly in our introduction, for the many believers who are unwilling to compromise our scientific knowledge, one approach is to say that we should not take Genesis 'literally'.

Then, if we are also unwilling to compromise a high view of biblical authority, we might re-interpret the Genesis 'days' for example, as long periods of time. The 'literal' sense of a day as a 24-hour period is altered and scientific knowledge retained, along with the Bible's authority, apparently.

It is not the purpose of this book to engage in detailed textual exegesis; we are concerned to get to a bigger picture for human language. I simply note that 'days as long periods' is not widely held to do exegetical justice to the term 'day' in the Genesis account.[18]

However, my main concern is that a significant driving factor for days as long periods is our material ontology, the lens of contemporary science through which some of us view Genesis. Here is an attempt to reconcile the creation account with modern science. It is our cultural background in which we are embedded and must try to leave behind.

Continuing with science, a different approach to the Bible's authority is to accept the more likely interpretation of 'days' as familiar 24-hour periods. We might then maintain the 'literal' sense by opposing the scientific understanding on cosmology and evolution with a 'literal' seven-day creation account.

While there are numerous unresolved questions around the scientific consensus, there is nevertheless an overwhelming consensus opposed by this 'young earth creationist' approach.[19] Again, I will not argue details but point to the theme of this book; we need to engage with the culture of the time.

Instead of doing so, the Genesis text is understood 'literally' and thereby in our familiar material terms, which then takes priority over contemporary science. Ironically, while seeking to do justice to the Bible's authority, this again is to impose a material ontology on the Genesis text dominated by the implications of contemporary science, even while rejecting that scientific consensus.

---

[18] See for example Wenham 1987, 19, 39–40. Walton also considers and rejects this day-age interpretation of the creation account. (Walton 2009, 90–91, 109–110)

[19] In the case of evolution, see Denis Alexander (2014), *Creation of Evolution—Do we need to choose?* A shorter section dealing with the relation of the ancient Near East is in Walton 2009, 107–109.

An alternative approach focuses on literary considerations which might then side-step questions of science. Here, we might see Genesis as a particular form of literature, employing metaphors or being a poetic account. While literary considerations seem plausible, we still need to do justice to the wider cultural context of the ANE.[20]

A variation on the above is to see Genesis as a 'myth'. The term refers to religious stories of origins involving the gods, where such myths play a significant role in the self-understanding of the peoples who hold them. The term readily evokes a fiction and may be used in a derogatory way.

However, given current cultural sensitivities, we try to avoid being derogatory, so the term might instead emphasise an important means to give and maintain a people's self-identity and their place in the world. Such a more nuanced sense of 'myth' has value in helping us understand the beliefs of a very different culture.[21]

Perhaps these literary approaches need not view the text through our own cultural perspectives. However, unless Genesis is set in a proper context, it will remain unclear what their understanding was, and how it might differ from our own. With these warnings about applying our own understanding to the text, we now turn to the context in the ANE.[22]

2.3 The Ancient Near East: Initial Comments

When believers read their Bible or listen to a sermon, it is likely they will be familiar with some of the kings and major kingdoms of the ANE: Egypt, Assyria and Babylonia. There were also the nearer powers such as Syria, Philistia and the more local tribal areas, which were a constant threat to the Israelites.

Commentaries fill out further details and may provide images of the major regional architecture like the Ziggurat, the Ishtar Gate of Babylon and other city

---

[20] Wenham concludes that "Gen 1 is unique in the Old Testament. In that it is elevated prose, not pure poetry, it seems unlikely that it was used as a song of praise as the psalms were. Rather, in its present form it is a careful literary composition introducing the succeeding narratives." (Wenham 1987, 10)

[21] A discussion of 'myth' is in Walton 2018, 33–34.

[22] A brief overview of all these discussed approaches along with some others is in Walton 2009, 107–112.

ruins which have been excavated. Statues and carvings of kings, gods and much else will also be illustrated.

However, for our purpose, more important are the deciphering and translation of the ancient languages and cuneiform writing. The rediscovery of Egypt grew from the eighteenth century and that of Mesopotamia in the mid-nineteenth century, the latter being our main interest.

The number of texts from these regions available to us today exceeds one million.[23] They include major myths and epics dealing with the gods and their deeds, letters of routine correspondence, divinations and incantations, royal inscriptions, chronicles, legal documents, hymns and prayers, wisdom literature, prophecy, instructions from officials, all of which give a valuable insight into life at the time.[24]

The important question for us is how the Genesis account relates to the wider cultural background where it originated. We should not think this background is a homogenous set of shared beliefs embedded in the social structures of the day. Varied influences came from invasions, trade and different kingdoms which waxed and waned while asserting the role of their own patron gods and origin accounts and also being influenced from elsewhere.

A good example are significant differences between Egypt and Mesopotamia.[25] Nevertheless, there were common elements which Genesis shared with the surrounding cultures. An important example concerned temples, which includes gardens as sacred space, divine rest and in the case of Solomon's temple, two groups of seven days for temple dedication or inauguration. Temples were also associated with the gods maintaining order in the creation, where the creation as a whole was viewed as a cosmic temple. Another shared belief is a three-tiered universe or cosmos.[26]

---

[23] Walton 2018, 3.

[24] Walton 2018, 12, 35–44.

[25] Various examples are in Walton 2018, 5–6.

[26] For aspects of the cosmos as a temple see Walton 2009, 71–100. For seven days being associated with temple inauguration and divine rest rather than physical building work, see Walton 2015b, 49–52. See 1 Kings 8:65,66 for two groups of seven-day celebration. Walton also notes the detailed analysis by Victor Hurowitz, who makes comparisons with similar practices in the ANE. (Hurowitz, 1992, 266–284) We deal with the three-tiered cosmos in Chapter 6.1–3; an initial comment is in Walton 2018, 10.

A further question is whether Genesis borrowed its material from the surrounding pagan beliefs. While this formed early scholarly debates, often for polemical reasons, latterly the interest has moved to looking at similarities and differences within a wider shared cultural background.[27] Our interest will also be with similarities and differences.

A summary of these points is by Gordon Wenham in his commentary on Genesis:

> "Gen 1–11 as we read it is a commentary, often highly critical, on ideas current in the ancient world about the natural and supernatural world. But the clear polemical thrust of Gen 1–11 must not obscure the fact that at certain points, biblical and extra biblical thought are in clear agreement."[28]

To illustrate similarities and differences, we turn to one of those widely held beliefs shared by Israel and present in Genesis. It concerns the nature of *existence*. I choose this as an entry to our theme of language by the giving of a name.

2.4 Existence and Giving a Name: A Functional Ontology

How did these ancient peoples conceive of something 'existing'? I will use terminology which is familiar to us with the caution that such terms must ultimately be understood in that ANE context. However, these terms are a helpful way into their culture. There are three aspects to existence in the ANE, all of which must be present for something to fully exist.

Separation. For something to exist, it must be *separated* out. This may seem obvious since we can hardly conceive of something existing unless it is distinct in some way from other existing entities. However, with Genesis, this notion of separation hits a problem when we ask what any initial created state might be separated from if the creation was 'ex-nihilo', out of nothing.

We will return to this question in due course. (6.4) For now, we note that 'separation' is conceptually necessary for something to exist in the thought of the ANE.

---

[27] Walton 2018, 10 ff.

[28] Wenham 1987, xlvii.

A Function Is Assigned. On being separated out, a *function* must be assigned to the not yet fully existent object. This is not a recognition of material-causal attributes or properties, but that a purpose or a role is assigned.

To say a little more about the term 'function'. For us, a planet will exert a gravitational pull, which is the *cause* of astronomical effects. We would not say that it is the *purpose* or *function* of the planet to have that effect.

However, the term 'function' can have that sense of purpose, particularly with our artefacts, the things we make: "The satellite *functions* as a communications hub; that is its *purpose.*" Such a sense of function as an intended role or purpose is the relevant sense close to the understanding of the ANE and used in the literature I refer to. Furthermore, given the priority of the function in the ANE, the previous separation should be seen as a functional separation rather than a material one.

To summarise, in order to exist, the separated-out object must have a role or purpose, which is the sense of 'function' we will use.

A Name Is Given. We might think that on being separated out with a function assigned, there is now a fully existing object. Yet not quite so. The object does not fully exist until a *name* is given to it. This might seem absurd to us. Surely, dinosaurs existed before there were humans to give the beasts a name!

Again, we remember that we are dealing with a very different culture to our own. Furthermore, this giving of a name is the entry I need to develop the language theme. However, we are not entirely detached from this ancient significance of giving a name.

For us to articulate that 'dinosaurs existed before humans existed to give them a name', we must name them without which we cannot make sense. To say 'X existed before' is meaningless if X refers to nothing in particular. The term 'dinosaurs' is as meaningless as the term 'X' unless the sense of the term is woven into human practices such as digging up their bones followed by careful biological classification.

Having seen something of that ancient sense of 'existence', there is one further step to take. How do we characterise the creation as a whole, as its components come into existence in the above sense?

Non-Order to Order. As its components come into existence, the creation moves from an initial state of *non-order* to becoming more *ordered*.

In Genesis, that initial state of non-order is characterised by darkness and water. It is probably unhelpful to call the initial state one of 'chaos' since to us the term suggests a falling away from order to less order, which in serious cases end up with 'chaos'.

For example, the result of an earthquake might be chaos or chaotic and some sense of order must be restored. While the term 'chaos' is a more appropriate way of describing Noah's flood, the term is best avoided in describing that initial creation state of non-order.[29]

A Functional Ontology. Needless to say, we must not confuse this progression from non-order to order with modern cosmology, where 'ordered' structures ranging from the atomic elements to planets and life on earth arose from some initial state or Big Bang.

Neither should we try to reconcile the Genesis increasing order with the Second Law of Thermodynamics! There is no common quasi-scientific model underlying the understanding of both the ancient world and our modern one. Hence, in contrast to the predominant material ontology which is the interest of modern science, we might call the beliefs and understanding of the ANE a *functional ontology* in that purpose-role-functional sense.[30]

That increasing order is a developing order of function rather than of matter. We note the contrast between the material ontology mentioned earlier, and this ANE view of creation as a functional ontology. However, we should not think the ANE was unaware or uninterested in the material of creation.

The point is that their concern was with the creation being ordered, and particularly that this order be maintained with the components of creation functioning as their role required within that overall order. A lapse back to disorder or non-order was a constant fear.

---

[29] I summarise too briefly Walton on 'existence', who deals with this at length in his chapter on Cosmology (Walton 2018, 147 ff.; also 48–53). An account of the flood was also common in that ANE, (Longman and Walton, 2018).

[30] I take the terms 'functional' and 'material' ontology from Walton 1015a, 23, 42–46; also Walton 2018, 134, 147 ff.

Walton summarises this in the following way:

> "In the ancient world, they were not ignorant of the senses and the level at which objects could be perceived by the senses. … The question here is not what they perceived, but what they gave significance to." [31]

Let's keep an eye on our direction of travel, though we have a way to go. In the ANE, to give a name, which is our linguistic interest, is part of something's existence as one thing rather than another (separation). To name is also to recognise a separated function which distinguishes one thing from another.

And finally, to assign a name is part of bringing something into a full existence, so that it can play its role or function in an increasingly ordered system. Clearly assigning a name is not a trivial matter in the ANE context.

2.5 Genesis 1 and the Enuma Elish (i): Examples of Ancient Near East Beliefs

Let's now illustrate that ancient way of conceiving existence, where the name becomes significant. The first few verses of the Genesis account and the opening of the *Enuma Elish* are good examples. The latter is a Babylonian creation myth recovered from the library of Ashurbanipal at Nineveh in 1849 by Henry Layard.

Ashurbanipal was king of the Neo-Assyrian empire from 669–631 BC and was probably responsible for freeing Manasseh from exile in Nineveh. (2 Chr. 33:13)[32] Following his death in 631 BC, Assyria came to a rapid end.

There are seven clay tablets and the text of the Enuma Elish is almost complete apart from a missing section of Tablet V. I will deal with the more familiar Genesis account first and then contrast it with the Enuma Elish, noting both similarities and differences. My purpose is not to give a detailed analysis but to illustrate the ordering of creation as separation, function and name along with some observations. We start with the Genesis creation account:

---

[31] Walton 2009, 25, also 34.

[32] A more detailed description of the library, its contents and Ashurbanipal's scholarly aspirations are in Frahm 2023, 290–297.

> "In the beginning, God created the heavens and the earth. Now the earth was formless and empty, darkness was over the surface of the deep, and the spirit of God was hovering over the waters.
> And God said, "Let there be light," and there was light. God saw that the light was good, and he separated the light from the darkness. God called the light 'day', and the darkness he called 'night'. And there was evening, and there was morning—the first day.
> And God said, "Let there be a vault between the waters to separate water
> from water." [7]So God made the vault and separated the water under the vault
> from the water above it. And it was so. God called the vault 'sky'. And there was evening, and there was morning—the second day.
> [9]And God said, "Let the water under the sky be gathered to one place, and
> let dry ground appear." And it was so. [10]God called the dry ground 'land',
> and the gathered waters he called 'seas'. And God saw that it was good."
> (Gen. 1:1–10)

In Genesis, that initial state of non-order is shown as water, darkness, formless and empty of anything else. Water and darkness are readily understood as having no differentiation; nothing is separated out. We should not object that the darkness is something distinct from the water; that is to impose a material ontology.

Water and darkness are that ancient way of portraying non-order where nothing functions since nothing is separated out to have a function in the sense of being there for a purpose or having a role which contributes to order. That was their functional conception; it is not a mistaken material one.

Then light is *separated* from darkness and *named* 'night' and 'day' by God. Though the function is implicit, it comes through clearly enough. Given that the coming creation of mankind is the crown of God's work, the function of day and night is that of marking time as the rhythm of human life.

The creation is being ordered into 'existence' in that ancient sense, in purposeful preparation for the creation of ourselves. As such the text gives the functional 'day' framework within which God also works to order the creation.

Since day and night are the basic rhythm of life for the coming humanity that is one reason to take them as the literal 24-hour periods familiar to us.[33]

There follows the separation of the waters above and below by a vault, partition or firmament followed by a further separation of water so that dry ground appeared.[34] These are named as 'seas' and 'land'. Again, the function is implicit but clear enough as the creation continues; this is the domain which will sustain life and in due course ourselves. Separation and naming are explicit.

The functional element continues with the installation of the heavenly lights in "the vault of the sky to give light on the earth, to govern day and night, and to separate light from darkness" (Gen. 1:14–19). The function-purpose of the animals is to fill the earth and of mankind to rule over the living creatures.

We also see the function-purpose of the plants as food. Most obviously with the creation of mankind, the man is formed from the dust of the ground while also being separated from that ground, and the woman from the side of the man. (Gen. 2:7, 2:21–22)

Here is another clear example of separation, with the function to procreate, fill the earth and rule it on God's behalf. The woman is named by the man and being in the image of God with the man, she joins him in that same function, sometimes called the *cultural mandate*. We return to our cultural mandate later.

In addition to these explicit examples, there are exegetical reasons for adopting this functional scheme, though we will not go into these.[35]

The point so far is to show the scheme of separation, function, name and increasing order as the contextual focus of the Genesis creation. To adopt a material-causal interpretation is to read our understanding into the text and fail to do justice to the cultural context of the time.

---

[33] See also Wenham 1987, 19.

[34] Several words are used to translate the Hebrew *raqiya*, the two most frequent are 'vault' and 'firmament'. The point is that the waters are separated for the purpose or function of providing a space for us and living things to dwell, with some kind of domed partition keeping the waters above in place. Walton concludes that *raqiya* refers to the space between heaven and earth with the waters above held up by a quasi-solid partition. (Walton 2015a, 159, an extended analysis is in Ibid. 151) We will use the terms vault, partition, firmament and sky interchangeably. The important point is to note the three-tiered cosmic structure. See also Wenham 1987, 19–20.

[35] Walton 2015a, 165–168; Walton 2018, 147–152.

Genesis shows the purposeful ordering of creation that it might function as a home for mankind in which we can then accomplish our purpose or function. We called this a *functional ontology* with the sense of 'function' being that of role or purpose.

There is one qualification to which we return in due course. A contemporary reader of Genesis may well accept the priority of a functional ontology. However, it does seem that some kind of structural element is not wholly absent. That is particularly so with the separation of the waters and what looks like a kind of quasi-solid partition holding up the waters above.

Indeed, we would judge such a structural perspective as mistaken. We will return to this in section 6.1. For now, we need to keep our focus on the ANE perspective.

The Enuma Elish

We next go to the Enuma Elish as an example which illustrates the wider cultural background within which Genesis is situated.[36] The opening to the Enuma Elish is as follows:

> "When skies above were not yet named
> Nor earth below pronounced by name,
> Apsu, the first one, their begetter
> And maker Tiamat, who bore them all,
> Had mixed their waters together,
> But had not formed pastures, nor discovered reed beds;
> When yet no gods were manifest,
> Nor names pronounced, nor destinies decreed,
> Then gods were born within them.
> Lahmu (and) Lahamu emerged, their names pronounced."[37]

---

[36] Walton applies this functional ontology to the Enuma Elish in Walton 2018, 50.

[37] There are differing translations, this one is from Dalley 2008, 233. This wording is also in Walton 2018, 50. The major Mesopotamian myths, including the Enuma Elish, are in Dalley 2008. A complete online version of all seven tablets of the Enuma Elish is in Mark 2018.

I have chosen this passage both as a comparison to the Genesis account and because of the striking prominence given to the name, which continues our major theme. First to clarify two terms: 'Apsu' is the god of fresh water with 'Tiamat' the goddess of salt-water. Both these two deities are closely identified with the waters. They effectively are the waters as well as personifications as gods.

Turning then to that primordial state of non-existence, we have waters mixed together, unseparated and undifferentiated. Pastures and reed beds were not yet formed or discovered, which again is that non-ordered primordial state. The importance of fresh water to these ancient peoples, its function, was not yet separated from salt-water and nor were the other land elements.

Pastures and reed beds also sustain human life, an implicit function. Other gods were not yet manifest. Given their close identity with different parts of creation, this is not surprising if that initial state is without differentiation.

While fresh water, pastures and reed beds are clearly important to these people, to what extent any function these have with respect to human life is unclear, given the marginal place of human beings in the Enuma Elish. However, since human beings are eventually created to serve the gods and meet their needs, the human function returns later.

The function of the gods in their control of creation is given in their 'destinies', which also were not yet decreed, nor were names pronounced. Hence, gods did not exist. Even Apsu and Tiamat are not yet separated; their waters mixed together.

Lahmu and Lahamu then emerged as separated from a primordial state, and with their names pronounced, they came into a full existence, their destinies or functions implicitly decreed.

2.6 Genesis 1 and the Enuma Elish (ii): Similarities and Differences

In the previous section, I made some initial remarks on Genesis and the Enuma Elish. Our concern now is with similarities and differences which show something of the common cultural background to both as well as where the Hebrews had a marked difference in belief. I confine myself to some obvious remarks.

Taking the existence scheme of separation, function and name moving from non-order to order, the Genesis account shows this clearly, with the functional element sometimes implicit, at other times explicit. The Enuma Elish is striking on the naming and explicit on function with the destinies of the gods.

Since the gods are responsible for controlling the various components of the cosmos and thereby maintaining order, the functioning of the cosmos is present. The initial state of watery non-order is present in both, Genesis adding darkness whereas the Enuma Elish has mixed salt and fresh water with no pastures and reed beds. Separation, distinctions and functions are absent in both accounts of the initial primordial state, which is one of non-order.

Differences are more striking, particularly with the nature of the gods. In the Enuma Elish, the gods are part of the cosmic system; they emerge from it or are born into it. The God of the Hebrews is not part of the system but is wholly distinct and has no beginning.

The details of the ordered creation in the Enuma Elish are less prominent than with Genesis since the main concern is with the gods themselves rather than with people in their relation to God. However, details of the creation of the cosmos are present, particularly in Tablet V of the Enuma Elish.[38]

Along with the polytheism of Enuma Elish contrasted with the one God of the Hebrews, the behaviour of those many pagan gods is not dissimilar to our own, possibly more disreputable, given their responsibility to maintain the order of the cosmos.[39]

In this connection, we mention Marduk, who was the god of the Babylonians and the central character in the Enuma Elish. In due course, Marduk does battle with the goddess Tiamat on behalf of the other gods and kills Tiamat. He is then given the rule over the gods and at the end, he receives fifty names, showing the scope of his rule.[40]

By contrast, Yahweh does not come into existence to receive any name or function, and does not do battle in order to rule; He rules and in due course reveals His names to us.

As for the creation of human beings, unlike Genesis, in the Enuma Elish, they are not the crown of creation but are made near the end, almost as an afterthought to serve the gods. They are little more than slaves to meet the needs

---

[38] Walton 2015a, 164; Walton 2009, 31–32. Numerous translations are available online, for example, see Mark 2018.

[39] Further details are in Walton 2018, 60 ff.

[40] For the Marduk's fifty names in the Enuma Elish, Tablet VII, see Dalley 2008, 273.

of the gods. The difference in human significance between the two accounts is striking.

We can take this further. The ancient belief was that the role of the gods was to control the different aspects of the cosmos, where the gods were almost identified with those aspects. It was of critical importance to those peoples that the gods should maintain order. An increase in disorder, or chaos as we might say, was a constant fear. Hence, serving the gods and meeting their needs was what mankind was made for; that was their function. And again, that allowed the gods to get on with their function of keeping order in the cosmos. It was certainly in human interests that the gods did so.[41]

The contrast with Genesis continues as the God of the Hebrews prepares this world for human beings not only to be in His image, but also to rule as stewards of the world on His behalf. And importantly, He will be with us. Hence, we see that God meets with the man and the woman in the garden.[42] (Gen. 3:8, 9) This is a very different relation to that of the gods of the surrounding peoples.

With other aspects of creation, Marduk makes the heavenly bodies to reflect the gods and thereby establishes time in years and days.

An interesting comparison is with Genesis where God separates water from water by a vault or firmament. In the Enuma Elish, the slain Tiamat, the goddess of salt-water, is split in two by Marduk like a fish, establishing a covering for heaven set against the deep.[43] There is at least some similarity with Genesis, though the means by which this happens are very different.

We might summarise that despite much difference in detail, particularly the character of divinities and the significance of human beings, there is a similarity

---

[41] For the creation of man in servitude to the gods in the Enuma Elish see Tablet VI. (Dalley 2008, 260–261) Concerning human significance and the meaning of life, Walton rightly notes that a material ontology cannot provide this. By contrast, there is a meaning to human life when related to the role of the gods, as the Enuma Elish does. (Walton 2015a, 43) However, that meaning still falls far short of the Hebrew understanding of the image of God in the Genesis account, as becomes clear later, particularly in Chapter 4.

[42] The temple complex was effectively a microcosm of the cosmos from where the god would exercise control and maintain order within their jurisdiction. There would usually a garden within the complex to grow the produce which meets the needs of the gods. A Ziggurat would also be attached to allow the god to descend to the temple. There are further similarities and differences in these beliefs, though not prominent in the Enuma Elish. Details are in Walton 2018, 73 ff.; 2009, 77–84; 2015a, 101–110, 178–190.

[43] Enuma Elish, Tablet IV, see Dalley 2008, 255.

in the cultural background, which is apparent in both Genesis and the Enuma Elish.

That similarity is also apparent in other myths of the time, though we will not take these any further. However, since our interest will continue with naming, we notice the significance of the name(s) of the gods. With the God of Israel, the names of God are intrinsic to His being and in revealing His names to us, we come to see something of who God *is*.

The prominence and significance of God's name throughout scripture needs little repetition. Just taking the xample of the Lord's prayer: "Our Father in heaven, hallowed be your name." (Matt. 6:9). Not only does the name 'Father' indicate our relation to God, that name and others are to be treated as holy, as is clear from the Third Commandment.

There is one final matter to close this chapter. Where do the principles originate which determine the ordering of the cosmos, the merits or otherwise of the gods and what are the appropriate destinies or functions?

For example, Shamash was the Mesopotamian god of justice and the sun, shown in the photo of the tablet with cuneiform text following. The god is seated above a sea with stars located below the sea and the solar disc prominent. [44] But what might be the source for the principles of justice which the god is to administer? It seems that these stand outside the system yet also determine the system and what should be the behaviours of gods and men.

There was an awareness of this question at that time and Walton notes the terms used in various languages. He makes helpful distinctions such as that

---

[44] The sun god Shamash, also associated with justice, is apparently seated above a sea with the stars beneath which may show the waters above the firmament. (Walton 2015a, 90–91; Walton 2018, 134–135) The description of the tablet in the British Museum also mentions resting on the heavenly ocean:
<https://www.britishmuseum.org/collection/object/W_1881-0428-34-a> Photo of the Shamash tablet by an Unknown Author licensed under Creative Commons CC BY-SA.

between the rules by which the cosmos works and the roles and functions of individual entities, which may be the gods.

However, there is still much debate about such matters, which may show this question was not developed in ancient thought. Again, the contrast with the God of the Hebrews is striking. Their God is not part of the system but sets the parameters by which it works where He retains ultimate control.[45]

We now have an overview of the shared cultural background in the ANE, which is essential to an interpretation of the Genesis creation account. The example of naming in Genesis is part of that ancient understanding of existence.

We have also noted other similarities as well as differences between Genesis and the beliefs of the surrounding peoples. The differences were most significant in the portrayal of the God of the Hebrews.

Furthermore, instead of our contemporary material ontology which we introduced earlier (2.2), we have what we might call a 'functional ontology'.[46] This is less concerned with material causes, processes or structures. Hence the Genesis creation unfolds the *purposeful* work of God to order the 'functioning' of creation as a home for mankind; that is the goal of creation.

That functional ontology was also present in the Enuma Elish and the wider ANE background, though again with very significant differences to Genesis.

The emphasis so far on context and the significance of a name is to prepare the ground for a wider perspective on language. The focus was also on the creative power of the name as part of bringing something into existence, which looks forward to the creative power of human language.

We must still do some further preparatory work to engage this ancient world from our contemporary perspective without imposing our perspective on them.[47]

---

[45] "The gods are 'in' the cosmos, and so, they are locked into certain parameters. How, when and by whom were these operational parameters established?" (Walton 2018, 58–60; also 161–165. See also Walton 2015, 46–62)

[46] I follow Walton's use with the term 'functional ontology'. (Walton 2015a, 43)

[47] Walton gives an extensive survey of the functional ontology of the ANE. (Walton 2015a, 23 ff., also 122 ff.)

3. Relating the Ancient to Our Contemporary World

We should take care not to impose our contemporary perspective on Genesis and thereby distort the beliefs of those ancient peoples. However, there are points of contact with our perspective. After all, we all live in the same world and are subject to the same physical possibilities and constraints, which arise from the way God has ordered His creation.

In this second preparatory chapter, we consider some of those points of contact to help us relate more easily to the cultural context of the ancient Near East (ANE). Having already introduced the term 'function' in the ANE and its creation stories, we start with our cotemporary use of this term. We should distinguish our use of term 'function' from the way we apply it to the ANE.

A closely related term widely used in the literature is 'teleology'. This is a very general reference to anything which is directed towards, or has a goal, end, purpose or function in that sense.[48] That may be the case with behaviour, our artefacts, living systems and some of their component structures, and possibly even non-living systems in nature. Some of our ways of using the term 'function' have a teleological sense.

After dealing with our contemporary use of 'function' and how it relates to the ANE, we continue with some analogies to further help us enter that ancient understanding of creation.

---

[48] 'Teleology' comes from the Greek *telos*, a goal or end of a period of time or a process. The term, along with related ones, are common in the New Testament.

3.1 The Contemporary Term 'Function': Cause and Purpose

An important point of contact with that ancient world, though also one which might be confusing, is the term 'function'. We used the term for the dominant perspective of the ANE's understanding of existence as a 'functional ontology'. A thing's existence required a 'function' as in a role or purpose, particularly in connection to the divinities; this is a *teleological* sense.

Our contemporary use of this term is not connected to any divine purpose; ours is predominantly a material ontology when we speak of something having a function. Depending on the context, there is some variation in our use and therefore also in the sense of the term for us. That is part of the creative power of language which can cause cross-cultural confusion, and even confusion among ourselves.

We should also not lose sight of our theme being language. Terms like 'function' and 'teleology' are effectively names, not of material objects, but of a rather more abstract aspect of objects or human and animal behaviours. A name has a wide and varied scope determined by a context of use, which thereby expresses different ways of understanding ourselves and the world we inhabit.

Turning then to our contemporary use of the term 'function' within a predominantly material ontology, Larry Wright's *Teleological Explanations* gives a helpful characterisation of a 'function' in our own use of the term.[49] The discussion which follows reflects a familiar way of speaking where we use the term 'function' in numerous contexts. However, it is worth putting this in more formal terms to distinguish the causal and teleological aspects of a function in varied examples, and hence to see how these two aspects interact.

To illustrate, in many cases when we speak about something, let's call it C, having a function, there are two aspects involved. There must be: (i) a cause, where C causes the outcome or result R. We must also be able to say: (ii) the cause C being there is *in order to* achieve that outcome or result R.

There is a causal aspect to C as well as a teleological aspect. If we have both (i) and (ii), we can then say that the *function* of C is to achieve R. That dual sense is one way that we use the term 'function'. There are other ways of using the term which we will also consider.

---

[49] Wright 1976.

To summarise, the function of C is R if we have both F(i) and F(ii) as below:

F(i): A cause **C** has the result or outcome **R**
F(ii): A cause **C** is there *because* it results, or *in order to* result in **R**

F(i) describes a causal effect, result or outcome and F(ii) gives a teleological perspective on that causal outcome F(i).[50]

However, we still need a justification or explanation for introducing the teleological perspective F(ii). Wright calls the justification an *aetiology*. This is a widely used term, where in medical practices it refers to the investigation of causes of a disease. As such, an 'aetiology' is also an explanation involving causes. Hence, Wright's sense of 'aetiology' is a justification for introducing F(ii) by considering the causal component F(i) in a teleological way.[51]

I particularly note that there is nothing strange or unusual about this cause, rather, we take a teleological perspective on causes where such causes are investigated by the relevant sciences or perhaps just everyday common sense.

This is best seen with some varied examples which show the term 'function' in contemporary use, followed by further discussion of these. In some cases, both F(i) and F(ii) are present, giving a cause with a teleological perspective. In other cases, F(ii) reverts to F(i) so that the term 'function' is now solely concerned with the causal. In yet other cases, the teleology is ambiguous.

1. The *function* of the heart is to pump blood around the body because F(i) blood circulation is a causal result of the heart pumping, and F(ii) the heart pumps *in order to* circulate the blood. The aetiology arises from the heart being an outcome of the evolutionary process where biological structures are adapted *in order to* survive in a particular environment. We also note the resultant complex causal and structural integration of the heart within the body, which we then perceive and speak about

[50] A similar formulation is in Wright 1976, 39, 81. These two components of a 'function' reflect a common way of speaking. While the two components may sometimes be muddled or ambiguous, we need to keep the distinction in mind.
[51] Wright 1976, 25, 37, 38.

teleologically.[52] In living systems, this functional terminology is even used with biochemical processes and molecular structures like genes and DNA.[53]

2. The missile is goal-directed or has a *function* because it locks onto the target which brings about impact F(i), and locking onto the target is in order to bring about impact F(ii). The aetiology arises from a complex of causes and causal feedback to achieve the goal, where missile components similarly have subsidiary causal functions F(i) and F(ii). Of course, we purposefully designed the missile and its functional components, which justifies the move from a causal to a functional-teleological sense.[54] This dual causal-teleological sense of a 'function' is common with our artefacts and is a further example of language woven into human practices.
3. The ozone layer filters harmful radiation F(i), but can we say it is there *in order to* filter such radiation F(ii)? We would say not; there is no aetiology within any science to support F(ii). We may say that the ozone layer *functions* as a filter in the ecological system. However, that use of 'functions' is no different from 'causes', given the lack of an aetiology to justify the teleological sense of 'in order to'. In this case, there is no obvious direct or practical contribution from teleological language to the

---

[52] Wright 1976, 84–87. The heart is mentioned by Wright along with other biological examples and natural selection. As noted previously, Wright's interests are with possible reasons for using teleological terms, which is different from the linguistic theme of this book, which seeks the creative origin of language in the 'speaking' of God.

[53] An extended online discussion of positions on teleology in biology is in Allen and Neal (2020). I am less concerned with the varied philosophical arguments on the subject. My focus is in the ability of language to enable us to see things in a particular way.
Denis Alexander also makes this teleological point with biology. He goes on to consider the varied sense of 'random' and 'chance', particularly in relation to biology and evolution, one example being the purpose of the giraffe's long neck. (Alexander 2018, 177) The point is that what we call 'chance' can and does work in conjunction with purpose, where again we see a teleological aspect.

[54] Wright 1976, 60 ff. Wright's discussion centres on reasons for a teleological perspective on the missile in terms of mechanisms, feedback and complexity. This book's emphasis in the main text is on language making sense by being woven together with human practices – we ourselves make the missile in order to hit the target. We are purposefully responsible for the mechanisms, feedback and complexity.

physical and ecological sciences, even if the ozone layer is important to life on earth. This is a case where F(ii) reverts back to F(i).[55]

Returning to biology, we can make a similar point. The crucial role of quantum effects in biochemical structures is more recent and becoming better understood. However, we do not say that quantum effects are there *in order to* enable biochemical processes and thereby life itself.[56]

4. The use of the functional F(ii) may be ambiguous. For example, the earthworm is a living system and as such, we would describe its structures as having functions in the sense of F(i) and F(ii), as with the heart earlier. But is the earthworm's function to aerate the soil, thereby having an important functional role F(ii) in the ecosystem? A farmer or gardener might say it has such a function F(ii), but others would say this is merely a benefit to the farmer or gardener, which is nothing more than F(i); the earthworm aerates the soil which benefits us. Any move to F(ii) becomes arguable but here, perhaps, the use of the term 'function' is ambiguous.[57]

Examples 1 and 2 above have a teleological similarity to the functions of existent objects in the ANE. In their case with creation stories, they prioritised the teleological function in relation to the purposes of the gods, with little interest in material causes and processes. By contrast, with cosmological processes we prioritise the causal within our material ontology with little interest in teleology.

Yet in some cases there is also a teleological perspective, as with the heart. The difference with the ANE is that our teleological use of function is not in relation to the divine but lies within a material ontology. However, a believer may well say that the ozone layer, quantum phenomena and physical 'fine tuning'

---

[55] At the time of writing, the overwhelming concern is with global warming due to levels of carbon dioxide in the atmosphere. However, carbon dioxide is an essential component of the overall ecosystem. The same question about the sense of 'function' arises as with the ozone layer. I will continue with the ozone layer.

[56] On the importance of quantum effects in biology, see Al-Khalili and McFadden's *Life on the Edge* (2014).

[57] An interesting case of functional ambiguity is the blood disorder of sickle-cell anaemia, which gives protection against malaria. The disorder certainly functions causally as a defence against malaria, but is that 'what it's there for' in the teleological-functional sense given the disability it produces? Again, any teleological sense may be ambiguous.

are *in order* that life and we ourselves should be here; these are indeed goal-directed by God. Doing so would get close to the ANE perspective.

Leaving aside any connection with divinity, an objection to this teleological form is that the aetiology is often vague and arbitrary. Clear reasons or arguments for a teleological perspective may be unconvincing.

More seriously, goals or outcomes might seem to influence the direction of causes, perhaps like Aristotelian 'final' causes.[58] This re-introduction of such teleological or 'reverse' causation is unacceptable to the sciences, particularly the physical sciences, which have spent much effort removing such reverse causation. After all, how can any functional purpose F(ii) drive the causal processes early on from a future goal yet to be achieved?

Another example of this functional-teleological approach being vague and arbitrary is that the heart throbs, so is the heart also there *in order to* throb! We would surely say not, even if throbbing is a useful indicator to check for a healthy heart. The same question applies to the ozone layer and quantum effects in the biochemistry of life; why should these not be described in functional-teleological way even though they are not so considered?

And importantly, who makes these judgements?

The answer is that *we* make those judgements even if clear criteria or arguments are not available. While such judgements are not arbitrary and may be supported or opposed, something of ourselves enters the way we use these teleological terms or names.

For example, we might argue that the heart's throbbing has no further significant causal effect. By contrast, pumping the blood enables numerous other biologically necessary processes to take place. This justifies rejecting the throbbing as teleological but is not a convincing argument against the heart's overall teleology. But then, the ozone layer filters out harmful radiation and thereby has in important role in the development of life, yet we still don't see it as 'teleological'. In making these varied judgements and the arguments which go along with them, our creative use of language in part forms our perception of how things are, ontologically, as we work with what we find.

---

[58] Aristotle thought there were four causes: material, formal, efficient and final. The efficient cause is similar to our explanation of causes in physical systems. The final cause directs something to an end. (Aristotle 1998, Delta 2, 15–117; Aristotle 1999, II.3, 38–42)

Furthermore, the teleological character of the heart is not just the opinion of some individuals. Teleological terms and the perceptions they form pose an awkward problem within the biological sciences:

> "There is an evident and uncomfortable tension within the biological sciences over the role that teleological explanations might play. Furthermore, if teleology cannot be eliminated from biology, this raises fundamental questions about the nature of biological explanation and the relationship of biology to the rest of science."[59]

Yet, it seems we can view biological systems teleologically without introducing novel teleological principles or explanations into science. This is shown in the way Wright remains *within* an aetiology of physical causes and processes while retaining a teleological view of them. That was the case with the example of the heart.

What then is the role of teleological language in those sciences dealing with living systems? Taking an example, a biochemist is not merely concerned with the properties of a biochemical molecule; she wants to know 'what it is there for', which is a teleological question about the function of the molecule in a living system.

But why this teleology when any scientific investigation is surely focussed on biochemical causes and structures?

One important aspect of living systems is that they are 'adapted' to the environment and have the ability to so adapt. It follows that we investigate biological organisms and causes within that overall adaptation which is 'in order to' survive in their environment. Indeed, the term 'adaptation' itself has a teleological sense as well as a causal-structural one.

Similarly, the components of a living organism, like the heart, are also set within and support that adaptation. The overall picture is similar to the missile, with the obvious difference that the missile is purposefully produced by ourselves whereas living systems adapt themselves.

Hence, with specific investigations into the adaptation of living organisms or the wider evolutionary process, this is a causal investigation within an overall teleological context. Even when the investigation is focussed on more specific

---

[59] Allen and Bekoff, 1998, 1–2. A similar but fuller online statement is in Allen & Neal, 2020.

processes and structures of an organism, for example to find the cause of a disease, such work still takes place within an overall adaptation to the environment. The teleological perspective remains in the background.

Put differently, suppose something 'goes wrong' with a living system because a biochemical causal process 'fails'. From the perspective of F(i), we cannot speak of anything 'going wrong' or 'failing'; there is simply a different causal outcome.

However, from the teleological perspective, it makes sense that something has 'gone wrong', which is not apparent from F(i) alone. Functional-teleological language is not so easily eliminated if we are to make sense. And hence, this language guides medical practices to deal with what has gone 'wrong' to put things 'right', which is that they function as they ought to.

We should note that the teleological-functional characterisation of living systems is within a complex of physical causes, processes and structures. This language in the biological sciences and with our artefacts is not concerned with any transcendent or divine intention or purpose. It arises from our predominant material ontology and is similar to our purposeful intentions in the things we make. Wright's teleological characterisation goes no further. In any case, God is not a special kind of 'cause' alongside material causes.

As we continue from here, we use the term 'function' in both a material-causal sense and with Genesis and the ANE, a divine purpose or intention while keeping these distinctions in mind. To help us do so, I will on occasions attach an appropriate qualifier to the term 'function'.

To summarise, our contemporary use of the term 'function' can have both a causal and a teleological aspect. This is part of a material ontology where the teleological aspect is our perspective on material causes. We apply this to living systems and our artefacts, though with the latter, we are the intentional agents of the teleological goal or purpose.

Furthermore, this variety of contemporary use is an example of the creative power of language embedded in human practices. It gives us a perspective, which is how things 'really are' to us, ontologically. It also shows a similarity with the ANE which makes our application of the term 'function' to ancient beliefs understandable, given that we also use the term in a teleological way in some of our language and practices. Nevertheless, our application of the term 'function' to the ANE relates the teleological to a divine purpose rather than material properties, causes and structures. That remains a major difference with contemporary use.

3.2 Our Artefacts: Separation, Function, Name and Order

Having mentioned our artefacts, the things we make, these show a remarkable similarity to the functional ontology of the ANE, particularly with their understanding of existence. Let's consider the invention of the wheel, since it appropriately takes us back to early days.

Allowing some amusing latitude in how this took place, we may be familiar with the cartoon where a caveman chisels a disk-shaped object with a hole in the middle from the surrounding rocks.[60] The cartoon leaves some doubt about what is to be done with this novel piece of stone, and even what we should call it.

We can use this illustration to show the ancient scheme for existence in our own artefacts where the separation, function, and giving a name leads to increasing order.

The chiselled disk-like object is first separated from the surrounding rock. Then this object gets a function-purpose to move things about more easily and efficiently, leaving aside the lingering doubt by one of the cartoon characters.

That is what the object is there for, it has that teleological purpose from ourselves. Finally, it is given a name, the 'wheel'. The result is an increase in order over the surrounding rocks as well as the role the wheel has in the ordering of human life.

We no longer speak of it as an unspecific object with an ambiguous existence, it now exists as a 'wheel'. And if we ask what a wheel *is*, we look at its *function* as distinct or *separated from* other functional objects and the original material we mined or otherwise extracted from the ground.

While this is an amusing illustration, we should not dismiss it. We have here a simple model of even the complex manufacturing processes of today, such as

---

[60] Vector Illustrator Moriz licensed from Shutterstock.

our earlier missile. Everything we make comes from the surrounding material environment and is separated out from there. And of course, whatever we make is for a purpose, or put differently, has a function in that teleological sense.

Even an ornamental glass object has a function, if only to delight us. In the case of our artefacts, it is fair to say that our intention to achieve that function is imposed on the artefact; the function is assigned by us along with a name.

We recall that when St Augustine was a child, he learnt the name of something, where that name was embedded in gestures and other social activity. The name does not float free from human practices which give the object its sense of being say, a chair.

The doing and saying are woven together, and so it is with all our artefacts. To apply this simple case more widely, the mining, planning, manufacture, marketing, finance and so much else are the myriad of human practices which give our named artefacts the sense of being what they are. The name, woven together with our practices which have functions within our lives, give us the sense of something being a chair, a wheel or a missile.[61]

In our contemporary understanding and practices, the material aspect is extremely important. We bring together the appropriate materials and knowing their properties after centuries of scientific progress, we make or manufacture sophisticated products to ensure the desired function is achieved.

There is an increase in order in the sense which would have been familiar to the ANE. However, while we have a good understanding of material properties and causes, the purpose or function of the artefact is at least as important as the material aspect. All that cost and effort is to achieve the desired function.

Hopefully then, our own practices make it easier to see the primacy of the function in that ancient understanding along with the importance of the scheme of separation, function, name and increased order. However, the difference with the ANE's creation stories is that the material aspect is also important to us, and rightly so since it is as much God's creation as anything else.

Indeed, we can envisage the cavemen in the cartoon thinking how they might improve the efficiency of the stone wheel—a wooden one perhaps? That means

---

[61] This way of putting it follows Wittgenstein's *Philosophical Investigations.* I am describing practices within human life rather than giving a philosophical hypothesis, theory or explanation. (Wittgenstein 1997, 47e, §109) Describing our practices, the saying and doing, leaves no doubt whether it is a chair, a wheel or a missile.

they will take an interest in the material properties, at least with their working products, even if not in the creation stories.

The point of the cartoon is to show that our artifacts have many similarities to the ANE creation accounts and their view of a thing's existence. There are also differences, such as the relevance of the name to something's existence, and particularly the ANE's lack of interest in material properties and processes in the creation stories. However, we should also remember that many of us are relatively uninterested in the internal material construction and electronics of our smartphones. We want to know how they function, that is, what they can achieve in relation to our needs and interests. That, at least, is similar to the ANE.

Nevertheless, we can fairly say that when the ancients were involved in a major building project, they paid considerable attention to the material construction. A good example is Solomon building the temple, where the material construction was important even though its purpose or function was the over-riding priority.[62]

In due course, we will need to return to the ANE and the material component of the cosmos. For now, let's consolidate these connections with another analogy drawn from contemporary life, with a greater emphasis on language use.

3.3 A Contemporary Analogy: The Language of House and Home

John Walton gives several contemporary examples to illustrate our ability to focus on a functional rather than a material ontology, despite our predominant material perspective. I will confine myself to one of his examples, with elaborations of my own. This example is particularly helpful in showing the different linguistic role of 'house' and 'home' terms embedded in our practices.

Walton draws the distinction between a *house* and a *home*. These again are closely related names referring to the same physical object but in different

[62] A key text on Mesopotamian temple building, particularly in contrast to the building of Solomon's temple, is Hurowitz (1992). The material aspect is very prominent in 1 Kings 6, 7.

aspects. These two names lead us to see the same object differently. We might even be much more interested in one aspect than another.[63]

We know that a *house* should have plumbing, electrical infrastructure and be attached to energy supplies on the external grid. The building will hopefully meet regulations on safety and insulation. When we move into a new house, we are aware of this infrastructure.

We know that everything in the house was made for a purpose, along with all the associated technology, which is their function. While such matters are of limited interest to most of us except possibly builders, electricians and plumbers, we are interested that it should all function reliably. A building survey should give us at least some assurances.

However, we are likely to be much more interested in how this new house will function as our *home* for the coming years. Which room will be the living and which the dining room? Which are the children's bedrooms? How will we arrange the lights and position the furniture? Where do we hang our favourite pictures to best effect and do we need to do some early decorating and change some of the carpeting?

Again, we are aware of material properties, (we want well-wearing carpets), but how these *function* as comforts, intimacy or the expression of a personal lifestyle, minimalism perhaps, is of primary importance.

The point of the analogy is that our concern is with the *functioning* of the house as our *home*, where the ancient Israelites were concerned with the functioning of the earth and its environs as their home, or better, the home for humanity.

There is a difference in focus between the house and the home. Similarly, there is a different focus on the way God orders material causes and processes (the house in our analogy) and the world functioning as our home.

This difference is also expressed linguistically with house and home language. For example:

House language: "Our new house has a heat pump which transfers heat from the garden into the house. Don't ask me the details; it is reliable and we just forget about it."

---

[63] Walton 2015b, 44–47. I have developed the details of the house/home analogy. Other analogies from Walton are creating a computer, the company and the restaurant. (Walton 2009, 24–25)

Home Language: "I love the way the curtains match the comfy furniture. The colours are striking and I always notice it when coming into the room. Friends often make a complement on it as well."

This house-home language and the functions of both house and home are inter-related. For example, we want the heat pump to achieve a comfortable temperature in winter since otherwise our enjoyment of our home is reduced. So, we set the thermostat. 'Comfortable' and 'enjoyment' is home language combined with 'thermostat' house language. Even so, there is a conceptual distinction with the interest in the home prioritised in this example; we set the thermostat *in order to* achieve comfort and enjoyment.

Let's take the home analogy further in meeting friends and family to strengthen those human relations. That the home should be inviting for meeting others is at least a part of its function. This home analogy points to one of the most important aspects of the ANE background.

A temple/garden is a microcosm of the cosmos from which the gods maintain order within their cosmic domain. It is also where the people meet their god to serve and meet the god's needs. The human-divine communion lacks love and intimacy in the case of the pagan gods, in stark contrast with the God of the Hebrews. Nevertheless, communion of the human and divine is part of the ANE's shared cultural background, along with important differences in Genesis.

Hence, Genesis has God meeting with the man and the woman in the garden at the cool of the evening. (Gen. 3:8, 9) This is about fostering the divine-human relation which takes place in the home of mankind—that is the purpose of the garden and ultimately the function of creation in the Hebrew thought of Genesis. Subsequently, that relation was closest in the actual temple building where God was present and met with His people.[64]

---

[64] For the significance of the cosmos and temple see Walton 2009, 71–91; 2015a, 100–121, 178 ff.; 2018, 83 ff. Walton notes the example of Solomon's temple and other examples of seven-day accounts. (Walton 2015a, 182; 2 Chr 7:9; 1 Kings 8:65) Temple inauguration concerns the functional-purpose of the temple, not its material build. Furthermore, the temple as a microcosm of the cosmos is not entirely foreign to us. Consider the soaring architecture of a cathedral. The function of the architecture is that we might more readily contemplate the transcendence of God as we commune with Him in the Cathedral.

Here again we can apply the house/home analogy, where now it is God who makes or orders the house to function as our home. When Adam and Eve meet with Him, the garden reflects the environs of a temple complex.

With the house-home analogy, we have a contemporary example which prioritises functional-home language, even though we are aware of the material structures of the house. Furthermore, when we speak about our home, the functional-linguistic structures and vocabulary of home language are significantly different from, but also related to house language.

We should therefore not be surprised to find the functional structure of Genesis creation account being significantly different from the material structure of the universe and life as we would relate it. For example, the way the Genesis days frame the increasing ordering of creation by God so that it is our home, is a functional framework of a cosmic temple which made sense to the Hebrews.

Those seven days are mirrored in the inauguration of Solomon's temple. (2.3) If the material processes of creation were not their focus, so it often is with our interests in our house, in contrast to our home.

However, as I noted earlier, the material may play some role in the Genesis creation account, since any function finds expression in the material. I will develop this point as we continue.

3.4 Ontology: Material, Functional or a Creational Worldview?

We have noted various connections between ourselves and the ANE, despite the way they prioritised a functional over a material ontology in their understanding of the creation. Furthermore, their functional ontology was related to the divine. By contrast, our contemporary use of functional language with our artefacts and in the biological sciences has a strongly material sense.

Hence, despite the similarity, we may still find it hard to see the Genesis creation account in transcendent functional terms. Surely the ozone layer does not have any divine-transcendent purpose or 'function' in that ANE sense, even if it does filter harmful radiation. We might be tempted to think like that.

If so, perhaps we can make progress by going in the opposite direction and allowing Genesis to speak into our context. In doing so, we join a transcendent-divine functional account to the material knowledge arising from our scientific developments. The result will then benefit both and without distorting either.

We can surely admit that our contemporary understanding of material properties, causes, processes and structures is far richer than that of the ancient world. However, scientific practices do not appeal to any transcendent-divine origin or intention, even with functional language in the biological sciences.

No scripture or theology tells us that $E = mc^2$. That is for us to discover by observation and scientific practices in the material world; the subtlety of creation is not given us on a plate.

Such is the case for both believers and sceptics, so that all can participate in the scientific enterprise regardless of religious or other beliefs. Some may even come to belief in a transcendent origin from the apparent design of creation, but we will not consider such a 'Design Argument', which is not itself science.[65]

However, for contemporary believers, the material aspect of creation is just as much part of God's work as any functional aspect; God's purposes are carried out within that material world. Through the eyes of faith, we can now see that ancient scheme of separation, function, name and ordering from both a divine-functional and a material perspective.

The ordering involves an incredibly subtle and complex organisation of the physical material and its laws making up the cosmos, or as we would now say, the universe.[66] The lack of interest of the ancients in a material ontology is enriched for us by our scientific knowledge. After all, the functional aspects of creation are observed within material structures, even for the ancients.

Since our overall theme is language, we should note how our developed theological language about a functional creation (our home) also goes beyond a merely material ontology (our house). Even so, the material has its place. This theological understanding arises from scripture where the different elements are put together:

---

[65] A notable example was the longstanding atheist philosopher Anthony Flew, who came to believe there is a God, given the fine-tuning and the cosmological development of the universe. (Flew and Varghese, 2007) For the application of explanations to the question of God's existence, see Richard Swinburne's *The Existence of God*. Teleological arguments and fine-tuning are in Swinburne 2004, 153 ff.

[66] Details of what is often called 'fine tuning' are in Davies (2006) and Zalasiewicz and Williams (2012).

> "For in him all things were created: things in heaven and on earth, visible and invisible, whether thrones or powers or rulers or authorities; all things have been created through him and for him. He is before all things, and in him all things hold together." (Col. 1:16, 17)

This is not a statement of material ontology; it expresses a transcendent functionality or purpose. It even includes a maintenance of the created order in that "in him all things hold together." However, the material of creation is surely present in that 'all things' and 'on earth' include the material. And supremely, the resurrection of Christ is the raising from the dead of his material body, as it will be for us. Transcendent functions find expression in material realities.

Finally, I need a new term to express our contemporary theological understanding, including its ANE context, along with our scientific knowledge. To speak of a material ontology does not do justice to the transcendent intention of God.

Equally, to speak of a divine-functional ontology might lose sight of the remarkable knowledge we have of the material world. And to speak of an 'ontology' may itself confine us to different ways of looking at existent objects through a philosophical lens. This again does not do justice to the all-embracing scope of creation.

Therefore, I will introduce the expression *creation worldview* to position ourselves in our developed New Testament theological perspective alongside our scientific knowledge. This accommodates the transcendent purposes of God and the Genesis focus on a divine-transcendent functioning of an ordered creation.

It also accommodates the knowledge we have of a remarkable material creation. It includes our use of functional-purpose language of living systems and our own artefacts. We do not need to muddle or distort either the Genesis functional account or a contemporary scientific account if we bear context in mind. Finally, to have a 'worldview' allows the widest perspective and the integration of all aspects of that creation without any distortions.

We also have a new *name,* which brings us see things in a different light, so we should next look more carefully at the name and its creative potential, which lies at the heart of this book.

4. The Creative Word: Adam Names the Animals

Having done the preparatory work, in this chapter we move into our main theme, which is a vision for language starting with a closer look at naming. We will also bring together some of the scattered points made so far. From the Genesis creation account, we turn to the man, Adam,[67] naming the animals.

What is the significance of him naming the animals?

This topic produces much hilarity. We imagine him sitting comfortably in lush pastoral surroundings. As the animals pass by, he is puzzled by what to make of that strange beast with the long protuberance out the front of its head. What should Adam call it—an 'elephant' perhaps?

However, only a moment's examination of internet images reveals no end of biologists making observations. We might come across Jane Goodall observing her chimps or David Attenborough taking us all over the world to show something of its varied and fascinating wildlife. Newly discovered species and behaviours are observed, studied and categorised, all of which are *named*. We need to take the Genesis account more seriously, though on its own terms.

The theme of this chapter is how our naming is a *creative* activity, which in a secondary and derivative way mirrors the creative speaking of God. There is no tidy single pattern to this creativity; we have an enormous variety in the ways we speak, only a little of which is reflected in what follows. However, I will try

---

[67] Wenham notes a play of words with 'ăḏām (man) and 'ăḏāmāh (ground) in Gen. 2:7 to emphasise the man's relation to the land. Wenham also notes that this wordplay is a favourite device of Hebrew writers, giving other examples. (Wenham 1987, 59) I will use the terms 'Adam' and 'the man' interchangeably as seems best in the context. For example, it seems right to use 'the man' when also referring to 'the woman'.

to do justice to the Genesis background in the ANE as well as contemporary knowledge by the following steps:

1. As Adam observes and names the animals, and assuming his naming is not confined to the animals, he comes to understand something of the function and order of creation.
2. As Adam names and thereby begins to understand the order of creation, he starts to exercise his rule, being in the image of God. This is part of our wider cultural mandate.
3. Being in the image of God, we relate Adam's naming the animals and thereby our naming and rule, to God naming the structures of His creation. This introduces a potential linguistic creativity on our part, which mirrors the creative speaking of God.
4. We close by considering how we might understand such a linguistic creativity of ours, and even give it a name.

I have introduced these cumulative steps since each one contains important points worth developing to build the picture of human language mirroring God's creative speaking.

4.1 Naming: Understanding the Order of Creation

In this first section, we see Adam develop his understanding of God's creation as he names the animals. What is he doing as he names them? [68] And are there similarities with our own practices as we name?

To start with our contemporary biologists, what are they doing in studying living systems such as animals? I have no expertise in biology but hopefully, the following superficial comment is sufficient to get us going. In the case of animals, I take it that one important aspect of a biologist's work is to observe how animals

---

[68] The purpose of this naming is that the man, Adam, comes to realise that there is no suitable companion or helper for him. (Gen. 2:18–25) Hence again in the wider shared ANE context, the purpose or function of the woman is prominent, rather than any material properties. The function of the man is also clear as the woman joins him as essential to populating the earth and ruling over it as his companion and helper. While this is the main point of the Genesis text, Adam naming the animals has further implications, which is our concern here.

behave individually and as a group within a wider environment. Biologists also study biological processes and structures. Put differently, biologists observe how in many ways animals and other living systems *function,* by which biologists then make distinctions between different or separate kinds.

As we have seen, this biological sense of 'function' can have both a causal and a teleological or goal-directed sense, but is not concerned with any ultimate transcendent purpose. (3.1) We might also say that the function of interest to biologists is part of a material ontology.[69]

We should not take the expression 'material ontology' in a derogatory sense. Biologists study living systems from this perspective and rightly so; it is a scientific approach extending our knowledge.

To continue, as biologists consider similarities and differences between forms of life, they make judgements on how living systems should be categorised. This is the *taxonomy* of life, a classification structured by categories, which are all *named,* as are the different life forms within a taxonomic category.

To illustrate this taxonomy, when mentioning Adam naming the animals earlier, by 'animals', we refer to the named taxonomic category or Kingdom of *Animalia.* There are five such kingdoms, with the most familiar being Animalia, Plantae and Fungi.

Sheep, goats and cows belong to the animal kingdom. These also belong to the Family of *Bovidae* lower down the taxonomic order. If we ask where the Alpaca fits, it is with camels in the Family of *Camelidae.* I make no attempt to explain the reasons for this classification, and accept the judgement of experts.

Returning to our original question, what is Adam doing in the Genesis creation account? It seems that he is doing something similar to our contemporary biologists. We might consider his role as *archetypal*, that is, an original model which embraces the many examples of which he, Adam, is the exemplar or archetype.[70] Those who follow as examples include our biologists.

---

[69] An early example of careful biological observation and classification is from Aristotle in his work *On the Parts of Animals.* (Aristotle 2004)

[70] Walton gives more detail on the archetypal role portrayed in Genesis by both Adam and Eve, the man and the woman. He also considers the archetypal role of Abraham, noting that an archetype can also be a real historical person. (Walton 2018, 178–79; see also footnote d. Also, Walton 2015b, 74–77)

Adam observes how the animals *function*, and thereby, *names* their different kinds. Furthermore, in naming the different kinds, Adam draws distinctions, or to use now familiar terminology, he notices the ways existing living things are *separated* from each other and separate from what is non-living or not an animal.

The evolutionary process seems a prime example of achieving such a separation within a material ontology. The resultant conceptual picture he builds up is that of an *ordered* structure, which reflects something of our example above—the taxonomy of life.

However, the reader may notice that I am subtly introducing what looks very much like a material ontology into Adam's naming the animals. Is this acceptable when the theme of the Genesis creation is located in the ancient Near East (ANE) where existence is functional, that is, within a divine-functional or purposeful intention? Our interest in material causes, processes and structures was not their interest when it came to accounts of origins.

So, if Adam names the animals within the transcendent functional ontology of the ANE, can we marry that up with our contemporary biologists and their material ontology without distorting either? How might we do this?

In the previous chapter, we considered analogies between our perspective and that of the ANE with many points of contact. We tried not to distort the one into the other but instead, we maintained the integrity of both. We also recognised that the material aspects of creation are just as much part of God's work as placing that creation within the purposes of God, which is its transcendent function.

Typology (Greek *tupos*) terms occur in the New Testament, being a pattern or example to follow. (Act. 7:44, Heb. 8:5, 1 Tim. 4:12, Phil. 3:17, 1 Thes. 1:7, 2 Thes.3:9, Tit. 2:7, 1 Pet. 5:3) We may or may not follow the example or conform to the pattern. An 'archetype' is not a scriptural term. However, it can make a helpful distinction between what we should or might conform to and what we actually *are*, ontologically as to our *being*. In our relation to the archetypal Adam, we are in the image of God but fallen due to our identity in the archetype. By contrast, in Christ, we are a new creation. The archetype reigns as it were as in "Nevertheless, death reigned from the time of Adam to the time of Moses, even over those who did not sin by breaking a command, as did Adam, who is a pattern of the one to come" (Rom. 5:14). In this case, there are also similarities and differences between Adam who, in this archetypal role, is a pattern (τύπος) of the one to come, Jesus Christ.

There has been progress in human knowledge, which was not available to the ANE. We therefore put both of them together in what we called a *creational worldview*. This does justice to the functional ontology of the ANE without distorting it, but also enriches the Genesis account with a better understanding of the material perspective of God's creation which we currently have.

We will now go one step further by noting that there is a latent presence of the material aspect of creation embedded in Adam naming the animals, even if the material was of little interest in the ANE creation stories.

To see this, let's give our imagination some leeway when reading the Genesis account. Within the wider ANE and also in Genesis, Adam's focus was that the animals have a transcendent function in the purposes of God. However, that will take Adam only so far in naming. For example, if I believe the elephant and the giraffe have a place in God's purposes that does not tell me that they are not predators like the lion say, or rodents like the rat.

Neither does it tell us that the lion is of the same family as our pet cat sleeping on the sofa, both being *Felidae*. We still need to make biological distinctions where belief in the purposes of God for creation cannot determine this. Rather, it is by scrutinising their material functioning as the biologists do, that Adam can make such distinctions and names accordingly.

While the text is not explicit, naming those animals must pay at least some attention to the material. Any transcendent function is expressed in the material and observed by interaction with the material. This is not surprising since the material is part of God's creation, even if the Genesis focus is on the functional ordering of creation.

Hence, a material functioning seems latent in the text, even if that is not the focus of the Genesis account within the ANE context. And again, that should not surprise us if we believe that Genesis is written within a cultural context but also speaks beyond its own context into ours.

As Walton puts it on numerous occasions: "It was written for us, but not to us."[71]

To summarise the different ways we have used the term 'function'. The perspective of a 'function' is a transcendent one in the ANE concerning the

[71] Walton 2015b, 19.

purposes of the gods or of God; we called this a functional ontology, which is less interested in material causes.

In our contemporary biological sciences, the term 'function' can also have a teleological sense, but within a material ontology which includes material causes, processes and structures. In addition, the artefacts which we make have a function, which is how they work causally alongside the purpose for which we make them. That again was the dual causal and teleological sense of a function.

But while Adam names within the transcendent functional ontology of Genesis, he implicitly recognises their material functioning. He cannot name without seeking distinctions in the material structures of the animals. Hence, we can see the transcendent and the material complementing each other and enriching our understanding of God's ordered creation in a creation worldview.

We also note again that the saying (naming) and the doing (observation, interaction with nature and the animals) are woven together. (2.1)

And so, Adam starts to understand more of God's order in creation. But what does that understanding contribute to Adam's function, as in his role or purpose?

4.2 Naming: Our Rule, the Cultural Mandate and the Image of God

Given the functional ontology of the Genesis account, we would expect that the man and the woman are also assigned a divine-transcendent function. This is indeed the case, as we saw earlier. They were to populate the earth and rule over it as God's vice-regents. (2.5, Gen. 1:26–28)

This rule should not be construed as brutal or selfish exploitation, but as careful stewardship to bring about human flourishing and the glory of God. We have seen it start as Adam names the animals and his understanding of creation grows. But what more can we say about that rule, and what has all that to do with naming?

In this section, we see that our function to rule arises from the man and the woman being made in the image of God. What does that imply? In the ANE, the image of God was readily understood since a king would be imbued with the image of their patron god.

Walton notes that: "Throughout the ancient Near East, it is usually the king who is seen as representing the image of God. That the king has been imbued with the image of the deity is the source of his power and prerogatives."[72] Walton goes on to describe, "The major responsibility of the king in the ancient world was to maintain order in that part of the cosmos he could affect; his kingdom."[73] As for people, they were there to serve the needs of the gods in a role not much different from slave labour.[74]

Here again, we see differences with Genesis. Unlike the surrounding pagan gods, the God of the Hebrews has no needs, which we then meet as slaves. Furthermore, while the surrounding kings carry the image of their patron god, with Genesis, all people collectively carry the divine dignity through God's image within themselves.

They thereby have a rule over the domain where they reside and even increase its order. This is surely an astonishing royal privilege and a complete reversal of the predominant ANE's view of mankind.

The perspective of a material ontology or contemporary scientific knowledge cannot give us that view of ourselves as being in the image of God. Neither can the sciences tell us what God's purpose for the image is.[75] However, being in the image of God, we can discern in our scientific knowledge something of the Creator's eternal power and Godhead. (Rom. 1:19–20) That we can and ought to do so is because we are made in His image.

The ANE sheds further light on Genesis. We have God resting from all His work on the seventh day of creation. 'Rest' is not as we understand it. To us, this would be a rest of relaxation, recuperation and an opportunity to catch up with some well-earned sleep.

But in the ANE, this would be when the patron god comes down to take up residence in the temple which people have made for their god. From the temple, the god maintains the cosmic order and exercises control and rule over their domain and is served by people.

So also, in the Genesis account we should view God's rest as Him coming to be in His temple, the created world. But differently from the surrounding ANE,

---

[72] Walton 2018, 184. Eckart Frahm describes the Assyrian coronation ritual around the fourteenth century onward written on a clay tablet from the twelfth or eleventh century BC. The ritual shows in various ways the close and near indistinguishable relation between the god Assur and the king. (Frahm 2023, 66)

[73] Walton 2018, 184, also 261, 186. An extended discussion is in Walton 2018, 256 ff.

[74] Walton 2018, 186. See also the Atrahasis epic. (Dalley 2008, 9, 14-15)

[75] See also Walton 2015a, 43.

He comes to be with us in the home He made for us, not the temple we made for Him.[76]

Then, as we fulfil our cultural mandate, God's rule is carried out in part by us as we increase the order in this world. God's rule is also carried out in partnership with us in the sense of that ancient 'rest'; God is with us in His temple, which is this world which He has given us to rule.

It follows that the image of God is not an obscure piece of theology. Rather, the image gives all human beings, men and women, a unique dignity and value. We will come back to value questions in a later chapter, for now the analogy with the image of the local king suggests we also have a mandate to rule, which is explicit in the Genesis account.

We are now in a better position to return to the question of naming. What was Adam doing in naming the animals, now from the perspective of being in the image of God?

If he, along with all humanity, is to rule and care for this world on God's behalf, he and we ourselves must be able to understand something about that world, at least to a level for us to carry out our functional purpose. That purpose is apparent from the Genesis functional ontology applied to ourselves—the image of God.

Hence, when Adam names the animals by carefully observing their structures, behaviours and adaptation to the environment, he comes to understand something of God's creation. And so, he starts to exercise his mandate to rule, as do our contemporary biologists in a much more developed manner.

In his archetypal role, Adam is not confined to naming only the animals and understanding them. He will be naming much more than that. For a start, he names the woman. Surely, he will soon be naming the stars and planets, the seas and mountains, the clouds and the weather, the plants and his crops, the endless variety of human relations and behaviours, giving proper names to his offspring and even that barely scratches the surface.

---

[76] Walton 2009, 71 ff. On the wider question of 'rest' in relation to the cosmos and temple in the ANE, see Walton 2015a, 100–119. Walton notes a variety of conditions giving rise to rest along with mechanisms and states of rest. One of these involves a state of sleep as well as others involving rule of different kinds. (Ibid. 111) Victor Hurowitz relates divine rest in Genesis to the use of 'rest' in the wider ANE. He notes a varied sense such as ceasing from intense activity as well as a sense of 'peace' as in absence of conflict. (Hurowitz 1992, 330–331)

As for the sciences, those who follow will take human understanding further and in due course name numbers and other mathematical concepts, physical forces, structures and processes to attain the range of scientific understanding we now have. We will also name values like good, evil, justice and beautiful. The terms' 'function', 'material', 'metaphysics' and 'ontology' themselves name philosophical concepts about the nature of creation itself.

But more is required. As all this naming is carried out and our understanding of the world grows, we also use this knowledge in creative ways. We make the tools to till the ground, build houses as homes to live in, make jewellery and other adornments, create music, art and literature and laws to attain a just society. Human language in all its variety is woven into our understanding and creative activity.

In other words, our mandate to rule is rightly called, or named, our '*Cultural* Mandate'. It is not merely about naming, understanding and ruling. Our mandate is the unfolding of the full panoply of human ability given to us by God. That mandate is for our flourishing and His glory by bringing further order to the creation.

While we have gone beyond Adam naming the animals, we are not dealing with some remote theological belief. As we see Adam's archetypal role, we also share in the function of the archetype and indeed, the image of God.

But we must take a further step. How does naming, and therefore language more widely, relate to the *creative* speaking or Word of God?

4.3 Human Creativity and the Creative Speaking of God

In this third section, we relate Adam's naming to the creative speaking of God, leaving us with a further question how far to take that creativity of ours.

We noted previously that to carry out our cultural mandate, we need to understand how the world functions, both in relation to God's purposes and in a material sense. Put differently, we need to know something about the complexity and variety of what exists, and we saw Adam start to do so as he named the animals. This is part of being in the image of God.

That image shown in Adam's naming takes us to God's creative speaking where God also names. As He speaks, there is an increasing order in the creation: "And God *said* let there be." A full existence is conveyed on what God has brought into being as He names: "And God *called*."

Here, we have God's creative word within that ANE understanding of 'existence' as separation, assigned function and giving a name, thereby achieving an increased order.

Then, as Adam resides in God's created world, he names the animals and in doing so, recognises how they are separated from each other and how they function in different ways. Adam names within that ANE scheme of existence which has its origin in God's own creative word and work.

He thereby perceives the order of creation. We also saw earlier that this ANE scheme is reflected in our own artefacts, the things we make. (3.2) There is human creativity not only in our artefacts, but also in the literature, the arts, music, science, engineering and so much else. This was the unfolding of the image of God.

Of course, there are also significant differences. God's work of creation is original in ways that our artefacts are not. Our creative activity takes place within what is already given in God's creation. Furthermore, God created what he saw fit to create without any advice from us. If He had created differently, we (if we were ever in such a different world) would have to work with that world rather than with the world we know. We might say our creativity is secondary and derivative to what God has created, and we create within the materials and constraints which give order to the world.

Nevertheless, we are creative and as we understand more of God's world, our creative capacity increases, as with the sciences and their applications for example.

But is there something deeper in the Genesis text? What else lies behind our creativity which shows something more profound about the image of God in ourselves?

God may have left us more room for our creativity, not just with our artefacts and what we see in human endeavours. The last explicit naming by God was on the third day with the 'land' and the 'seas' (Gen.1:10). Following Walton, I have taken these to be the major functions of time, space and the location for our lives.

After this, there is further structural ordering as with the vegetation, the lights in the vault of the sky and the living creatures, yet without additional explicit naming by God. Certainly Genesis refers to these created components, otherwise the text could not make sense. Yet the naming by God seems absent. Is there perhaps something still missing from a full existence of these later elements of creation?

This might seem absurd to us, but we are in the context of the ANE where such a lack of full existence in their understanding may not be so absurd. Perhaps there needs to be a further act of naming to bring the creation to completion, which will come from us, being in the image of God.[77]

That brings us yet again to Adam and those animals.

We have seen that Adam is not merely a human person giving things a name; his naming needs to do justice to the image of God. God has already created and named the major components required for our existence: time, space and the land and seas on which we will live. Then we find Adam naming the animals, and presumably, he will soon name other elements of creation.

Finally, as he sees how the animals function and names them accordingly, he recognises there is none to function as a suitable helper for him. God separates the woman from his side to be that helper.

Adam recognises that both he and the woman whom God made from his side are different from the animals; together they share a special purpose. He recognises her purpose in God's ordering of the creation in being like himself and alongside himself. The man then names the woman accordingly: "This is now bone of my bones and flesh of my flesh; she shall be called 'woman', for she was taken out of man." (Gen. 2:23)

Here that ANE priority of the functional over the material is again clear, while not losing sight of the material subtext—bones, flesh. For the function of both the man and the woman to rule, procreate and fill the earth the material aspect is implicit, even if it is not the Genesis focus.

We saw earlier that a similar situation arose with Adam naming the animals, where the material was implicit. (4.1) Then finally, as the man names the woman, that is a further step in the ordering of creation.[78]

But if our artefacts and so much else we do and make is creative, it is not clear what is creative in Adam *naming* those animals; surely they simply are what they already are. Similarly, naming the woman does not change what she

---

[77] Walton distinguishes between the functional components of creation followed by the installation of the 'functionaries'. (Walton 2009, 62–70)

[78] Wenham notes both the equality of the man and the woman, along with the expectation of her subordination and its result. (Wenham 1987, 71) The consequent treatment of women is a long way from God's original intention. This is not a major theme of the book, but we should at least note Wenham's comment in regard to the many corruptions in the function of the man-woman relationship.

already *is*. Even if God's naming activity stops in day three with the land and seas, what is so creative about our naming the subsequent parts of creation?

The constituent objects and structures are what they are and there is nothing we can do about that! Careful observation is admirable and necessary to recognise this, where scientific practices are certainly creative in their own way. But none of those practices changes what is already there, neither is anything brought creatively into existence just because we name it. The elephant is an elephant and not a giraffe, whatever we call them, and both belong to the *Animalia* Kingdom.

Surely that is obvious. As Juliet said: "What's in a name."

So, it seems our creativity stops with what we make in our artefacts from the material that is already present; our creativity does not extend into the world which God has already created. We might be mistaken as to *how* that world is, but that is for us to correct as we develop our knowledge. After all, our knowledge of God's creation is only *knowledge* when it reflects how things *are*, which is how God made them, so we might suppose.

Nevertheless, I will question the above and take a different approach. Certainly, we exercise creativity in what we do and make, and also in literature and everyday speaking. But here we are looking at naming parts of creation. Adam is naming the animals where in the thought of the ANE, naming something brings it to a full existence. Furthermore, God brings the animals to Adam to see what Adam would name them. God then confirms that name: "And whatever the man called each living creature, that was its name." (Gen. 2:19) If this is in some way creative as to the animals' existence, that may say a great deal about other areas of human creativity.

We next look at a possible creative aspect in naming the animals, which in a secondary and derivative way reflects something of God's own creativity as He names. There may be more to the image of God than appears at first sight.

4.4 Creativity: Reflecting or Constructing Reality—or Both?

Let's start by asking how Adam's naming relates to what God has created. We might answer that when Adam names, he places a verbal label as it were, on something that is already what it is since God created it to be that thing.

We saw earlier that Adam noted distinctions between the animals as part of the varied order of creation. (4.1) In a material ontology, we now call this the taxonomy of life.

The question here is not that he notes their differences and names them accordingly. Our question is whether Adam himself makes a contribution of his own to how he perceives and judges their functional similarities and differences in the process of naming. And what might be the status of that contribution of his in the way he (we) perceive things to be one kind of thing rather than another?

We first look at the case for 'labelling' what is already there. Since God made those elephants, Adam need only see how their structure and functioning is distinct from the giraffe say. He then names (labels) those animals with the name 'elephant' distinct from 'giraffe'. And of course, both are animals rather than plants. Hence, the taxonomic categories are a question of recognising and then labelling, or we might even say 'mirroring', what is already there, because that is how God made it. In ANE terminology, that is how God has ordered the world.

To use a now familiar philosophical term, the ontological distinctions of creation are unaffected by the way we name, and our naming should reflect the created and ordered existing ontology.

This is a good example of the metaphysical model, which goes back a long way and is still influential. Aristotle gives a classic statement of the relation between language and its symbolic relation to the mind and that already in-place reality which language and mind represent. At the start of *On Interpretation,* he writes:

> "Words spoken are symbols or signs of affections or impressions of the soul; written words are the signs of spoken words. As writing, so also is speech not the same for all races of men. But the mental affections themselves, of which these words are primarily signs, are the same for the whole of mankind, as are also the objects of which these affections are representations or likenesses, images, copies."[79]

For Aristotle, *the objects* of which these affections are representations constitute that reality which is other than ourselves but is the same for us all. This model also shows the danger of those objects becoming detached from human

---

[79] Aristotle 1938, 115.

life, creating a 'metaphysical gap', which then needs to be addressed by some metaphysical theory.

However, for the moment our concern is with the symbolic labelling of those objects corresponding to our experienced mental affections, which are the same for us all. That is one way of understanding what Adam does when he names those animals. The 'elephant' is an elephant for us all, as is the corresponding mental picture or impression, though the names we give as verbal sounds vary and are ephemeral.[80]

In this labelling model applied to Genesis, there are *essential* ontological distinctions previously created by God as the ordered structure of creation. It is our business to recognise this in our naming practices. Hence, it seems the structure of reality determines our naming schemes and beyond that, our language in speaking about the world.

In philosophical terms, this is usually called, or named, 'essentialism'. Another often used name is 'realism' where our senses put us in touch with reality as it 'really is', which is also the ontological question. Since this labelling model has a ready intuitive appeal which we tend not to question, it is also called 'naïve realism'. We name things directly as they really are. [81]

But we might take another approach. As Adam makes his observations, *he* judges what functions or structural features are relevant to the separateness of one animal from another, and one kind from another. Among the enormous, complex and sometimes subtle variety which is part of this created world, he must judge which aspects matter most, matter less or are irrelevant.

---

[80] The metaphysical vulnerability of this model is apparent as Aristotle's words echo into our time. Jacques Derrida quotes him in a section where Derrida argues that 'rationality' no longer issues from a logos. The result destabilises both meaning and truth. (Derrida 1976, 10–11) While his language is convoluted, it is nevertheless clear enough. In our case, a metaphysical model for Adam naming the animals is directly related to God, Derrida's logos, which has now come to an end. (Ibid. 12–15) The metaphysical model in the main text, underpinned by God, gives stability to Adam's names for the animals. The loss of the divine Logos leads to Derrida's de-construction along with the whole Genesis metanarrative and its 'truth'. Even biology may not be exempt.

[81] There are variations on this *essentialist* or *realist* metaphysic. The relation between words in a language might reflect the structure of reality with an analogy of a picture relating to what it is a picture of. This is the theme of Wittgenstein's earlier *Tractatus* (1974). Again, this leads to a crisis since we can't obviously 'picture' ethical or religious beliefs.

This is not just given to him on a plate by God through the creation; Adam is responsible for making those judgements as he names the separate kinds of animals. The biological taxonomic classification is again a good example.

Let me develop this point through a personal anecdote.

There was an occasion when my wife and I went on an Arctic cruise. The ship was of the smaller variety with plenty of opportunity for trips ashore on the Svalbard islands and subsequently in Greenland. The passengers were accompanied by a team of biologists and other experts in the local flora and fauna.

At one point, I asked a biologist a question about the taxonomic classification system. My question was whether this taxonomy described the reality of the way living systems were structured; was that their structure 'in reality'? After a short hesitation, the answer was along the lines of: "Yes, that is how life really is structured." It was an 'essentialist' or 'realist' answer.

The hesitation was probably due to the question being a philosophical one rather than a biological one. Sometime later, I went to another biologist with the same question, whether the taxonomic categories described the reality. This time the answer was instant: "No, it's a construct of ours."

So, what was Adam doing in naming the animals? Was he merely labelling the reality as it already is, or at least in part making a constructive contribution of his own as he named? Certainly, the creation is ordered, but in this constructive model, Adam's understanding of that order is based on judgements he makes as he considers the factors which he thinks are relevant, and hence the order for him is partly as he construes it.

He thereby *constructs* his naming scheme as it were, which is called 'constructivism'. The results are his 'constructs', which are part of his understanding within the cultural mandate. To Adam, and to ourselves, the ontology of existence is in part constructed by ourselves.

A good biological example would be our earlier case of the heart's function having both a teleological and a causal-pumping component. We noted that this leaves some awkwardness in the relation of the biological sciences to the physical sciences since teleology is not acceptable to the latter. (3.1)

We also recall that the heart causally throbs, but the throbbing is not taken to be part of the heart's purpose as is the pumping. It is we who make those distinctions and hence the constructing on our part, in this case our constructing the heart's teleology.

Adam might have approved. [82]

I have deliberately qualified this constructive approach in various ways; it is not arbitrary or entirely subjective. Our constructions are only 'in part'. We recall that God has named the major structures of creation which are thereby given to us all. Furthermore, those structures are pervasive in the material world.

Some cultures may have a very different approach to time from our own, but the reality of night and day is unavoidable. For example, we are all affected by reduced visibility at night. The seasons govern crop planting and harvest for everyone.

Many peoples have had a geocentric view of the heavens, but we can say this is mistaken not just because we now have scientific knowledge, but because God has ordered it so, with that ordering being named. Since that ordering pervades the creation, our naming will be constrained, may just differ from how other cultures name or may be mistaken.

The point overall is that Adam makes judgements about what is relevant to the separation and functioning of the components of creation. He does this as he names and that is how things appear to be for him. It is part of his role to rule on God's behalf, which God will uphold. However, Adam's constructions of how things are do not float free from a creation ordered by God.

There is an important qualification to Adam's constructing; the being of God Himself lies outside the creation, unlike the pagan gods. Hence, God is not a subject of Adam's constructions since God is not an item in this creation alongside everything else. God is not within the domain of Adam's rule, though that happens too often as human beings construct the divine in their own image.

Put differently, the being of God is not a personal, social or cultural construct, even if different religions or secular cultures construct this differently. There are other matters which are also not in Adam's domain, such as the image of God in human beings and that our cultural mandate is given by God.

---

[82] In dealing with natural theology, Alister McGrath notes that the natural world does not directly 'speak' to disclose its own meaning or significance. "The construction of meaning is the creative work of the human mind, as it reflects on what it observes." While nature might point to its meaning through its structure, "the identification of that meaning lies with the observer, who must construct a schema, a mental map, in order to make sense of what is observed" (McGrath 2009, 4). This twofold aspect, our constructing a mental map which makes sense of an observed structure, is also the theme of this section and recurs elsewhere.

These also may be constructed differently in different cultures, with slavery and the marginalising of women being examples. Hence, if Adam is to relate truly to God and to other human beings given their significance, he will have to rely on God's revelation of Himself and His purposes, not on his, Adam's, own constructions.

This is one of those occasions when philosophy intrudes itself into the creation account, which is helpful at least in clarifying the point at issue. Both the essentialist-realist and the constructionist face different though significant problems. Perhaps the most serious for the essentialist is *how we know* whether we have a true description of the reality.

How can we truly describe and name a reality that is other than our sensations, conceptions and even our scientific theories? That is a classic metaphysical question where one of our examples was the biological taxonomy. If philosophical theories do not resolve this metaphysical question, and it is doubtful that they have, it may not be a good idea for us to introduce a realist model into the creation account. And without a realist model, what can we ever say or know about 'reality'?

Which brings us to the constructionist.

Since different individuals, groups and cultures may construct their understanding differently, the major problem for the constructionist is that of relativism in relation to truth. Related to that is another awkward question: on what grounds might we reject the predominant beliefs and practices of other cultures if these are merely constructed differently from our own? Perhaps both the metaphysical and relativism question are two sides of the same coin.

We will consider these in chapter 6, when dealing with some important objections and challenges.

To close this chapter, I re-emphasise an important point. I will take the construct model further since it gives a route into the creative aspect of naming and language more widely. It thereby does justice to the image of God. However, we must not lose sight of this taking place within a creation which has been ordered functionally *and* materially by God.

Some of the major orderings of creation in days one to three were also named by Him. It is therefore likely that some of our constructive activity in understanding creation will converge, which is particularly striking with the physical and related sciences.

What God ordered and named in those first three days underpins everything else. The subtlety of the laws of nature and fundamental physics are examples which were not known to the ANE and are not part of the Genesis account. That the planets go round the sun is another example which surely is not merely a construct of ours! And if any people or culture think differently, they are mistaken.

However, perhaps not even all our scientific knowledge is quite so secure as that. So, I will not be overly dogmatic on the construct and realist approaches which are not entirely separable. That should not surprise us given the subtle complexity of the creation which will constantly astonish us, while we must also achieve a straightforward understanding to survive and at least start to rule.

This question of our constructs working within the constraints of God's ordered creation and within scripture will return at various points and we must not lose sight of it. It is a wider application of our saying and doing being woven together in order to make sense, as we saw with St Augustine learning the name of something (2.1).

So, while not forgetting the above point, I will next illustrate our wider linguistic creativity with an emphasis on the constructive aspect, which takes us to the next chapter.

5. Creativity and the Construct Model: Examples

We continue with the construct model. However, I will not attempt a precise explanation or definition for this term, nor will I wrap it in a theory. Instead, differing examples will illustrate the wide range of our linguistic creativity, which is too rich and varied to be neatly contained in some theoretical model.

The term 'construct' and our 'constructing' are broad-brush terms to direct us to particular instances of our varied linguistic practices. The examples which follow will not do justice to that rich variety.[83]

Nevertheless, there are three important themes running through these examples. I am bringing together (i) a context of human life, (ii) that life of ours lies within a creation ordered by God and, (iii) something of ourselves and our judgements enter into our linguistic practices, which thereby forms our understanding.

Though these three themes have appeared previously, we must not lose sight of the scriptural background. Underlying the following examples is the archetypal Adam. As he names the animals, he notices differences and similarities, and thereby groups them according to their kinds.

But it is Adam who judges what features are relevant to how he categorises and names; his judgements determine the names. Hence, how Adam names these animals also become what they are for him, reflecting his rule in the image of God and the role of the name in the ancient Near East (ANE) scheme of

---

[83] Jonathan Potter, in his aptly named *Representing Reality* (1997), shows something of the enormous variation in the construction of meaning, both in relation to personal interest and science. This book is not concerned with that variety but with the origin of our linguistic creativity in the image of God and the cultural mandate mirroring God's own creative Word. My few limited examples are just intended to illustrate my theme. I refer to Potter in more detail in 6.5.

‘existence’. There is a creativity which mirrors in a derivative and limited way the creative speaking of God.

Similarly, in the following varied examples, we try to see how our own judgements contribute in different ways to how things are for us. We cannot entirely detach ourselves from our judgements to gain a wholly person-independent or objective viewpoint.

Our judgements are also formed and influenced within a complex mix of social beliefs and practices; our perspective is not merely a personal matter. Additionally, our perspective can be formed by wisdom and some self-criticism, which we will look at in due course.

Finally, because our judgements are rooted in human life within a world created and ordered by God, there are constraints. In some cases, such constraints enable us to appeal to ‘the facts’. Hence, there is scope in some areas to investigate and come to realise we were mistaken as to the truth.

The following examples show in different ways how our creative constructs interact within God’s creation, and that our judgements also need to work with our critical and investigative faculties—and with scripture. Those critical faculties of ours are also part of the image of God.

Doubtless many other factors affect our judgements in examples which follow, but I trust the discussion below is enough to show our linguistic creativity.

5.1 Metaphors (i): Juliet’s Rose

Metaphors are pervasive in human language and play an important part in its creative power; they are not merely literary devices to achieve some effect. We now turn to examples where what is familiar becomes a metaphor for deeper human concerns.

The familiar can be used as a metaphor to convey to us the reality of something else as it were, where again the name plays an important role. What ‘conveying a reality’ might mean is what I will try to draw out from the examples which follow.

We started with Shakespeare’s Romeo and Juliet, where Juliet says: “What’s in a name? That which we call a rose by any other word would smell as sweet.” The rose and its sweet smell are metaphors which Juliet applies to Romeo and her love for him.

Even if he had a different name, their love would remain the same because he would still be the same person, just as that rose remains a rose, whatever we call it. Of course, Romeo is not a rose, his name is not that of a rose and Juliet's love for him is not an appreciation of a rose's sweet smell.

The literal rose, its name and sweet smell are used metaphorically for the person, Romeo, the love Juliet has for him, and his enduring person being different from his ephemeral and arbitrary name.

We can also say of some metaphors that they are *true*. However, Juliet's metaphor is not literally true as if Romeo is actually a rose. Neither is Juliet making an everyday statement about the smell of a rose. Romeo and Juliet, along with ourselves, correctly interpret the intended metaphorical sense that just as a rose's sweet smell is the same whatever the rose is called, so Romeo is the same person whom she loves whatever his family name may be.

When standing in a garden perhaps, we might appreciate the rose and its sweet smell literally as experienced directly through our sense of smell. Indeed, that must be so in order to appreciate the metaphor in Juliet's lived context of family enmity and her metaphorical application.

Hence, the truth of a metaphor is related to its context of application and the point it is intended to make rather than a literal truth, though the metaphor may ride on an experienced literal truth.

So, in that metaphorical sense, is Juliet's metaphor *true*?

At first sight, we might agree with Juliet. Romeo is that enduring and substantial person whom she loves, whereas the family names are surely mere ephemeral and arbitrary labels which might have been different. A name cannot literally of itself be an enemy; the enmity is between the persons of the two families and not in their names as such, which might well have been different. All this seems merely obvious and in Juliet's metaphorical sense, true.

Yet, we are now moving from the metaphor to a rationalisation which underlies the metaphor, with the metaphor being convincing enough to confirm the reasoning. But ironically, as Juliet denies the power in a name by means of the rose metaphor, she tacitly acknowledges that names do have power.

For a start, she uses the highly effective rose-*named* metaphor to express her love despite her wishful thinking that the rose's name is irrelevant to its sweet smell. Nevertheless, it is that name 'rose' which directs her and our attention so effectively to the flower's beauty and its sweet smell.

Hence, the metaphor derives its effect partly from the name evoking that sweet smell. Ironically, she then experiences the power of the name by the enmity conveyed through the family names, which she denies.

One might argue that the family names are little more than labels and so have no substantive significance. However, as names they convey a reality of enmity just as does the rose-named metaphor conveys a reality of love, and even evokes that sweet smell. To say 'She's a Capulet' would be insulting and damaging to Juliet in the view of the Montagues and their friends, given the family feud.

And so, Juliet's use of the metaphors to separate the person from the name is doubtful. Even if the names of the families and also the rose were different, the rose's smell and the family enmity would still be conveyed, though by different names.

That is because the name, whatever it is, is embedded in a context of human life and derives its influence from that lived context. Again, the saying (the name) and the doing are woven together in our lives from where that name, whatever it is, derives its meaning and its influence.

Given the context where Juliet experienced that power of enmity, her words undermine themselves as it were. "What's in a name?" A great deal it seems. Some might be delighted with the irony of the text deconstructing itself!

But perhaps Shakespeare wants us to consider that words and names are more powerful than we sometimes wish, after all, he is the master of using words to enduring effect. Indeed, the names 'Romeo and Juliet' still echo their love with us today, despite them not being real persons but fictional characters.

More generally, a well-chosen complementary epithet is appreciated while a hostile one can be devastating. To adapt a well-known saying: 'Sticks and stones can break my bones', but names can be even more destructive. Devising a name seems to be a particularly valuable political skill, which is hardly news given our theme so far.

A name may convey a reality or just evoke one with great effect, which applies to Juliet's experience of those family names as well as her metaphorical rose.

One might wish to draw a distinction between a metaphor conveying or even embodying something and merely evoking it. To evoke suggests only that thoughts and emotions are raised rather than anything more substantial being conveyed. However, it is precisely those thoughts and emotions which form the enmity Juliet experiences as if it came directly from the Montagues in person.

To continue with metaphors, suppose Juliet said more prosaically: "What's in a name? Romeo is the same person I love whatever his name." While this is doubtless true as to their love, it is a hardly a memorable statement. More significantly, being rather mundane, it fails to convey Juliet's love with the intensity she felt, which comes across more strongly with her original rose metaphor.

A metaphor may be more effective in conveying something of importance than a humdrum literal statement. We might even say the metaphor is *more true*, in the sense of being more effective and richer in meaning than the prosaic statement. That is one reason why it is so compelling.

Let's make this point differently. The term 'love' is in the prosaic statement above, but what does it mean? Can we really explain this effectively in yet more everyday words than by the metaphor of a rose's smell? The strength of these emotions is hard to convey with literal statements because they are not wholly literal matters 'out there'; they are 'in here within ourselves' as it were.

The smell of the rose immediately connects with our sensations and internal feelings. Again, truth may be conveyed more effectively by metaphor than literally, but then, so may a misleading tendency and an outright falsehood. We will return to this question of deception or error shortly.

Finally, on being creative, the rose metaphor is chosen for its associations with the sensation of smell and the pleasure which that smell gives. It is Juliet's *intentional construction,* though other metaphorical constructions might work just as well. The effect on the hearers is highly effective since it taps into human emotions which we share.

A well-chosen/constructed metaphor derives its effect from its connections with other parts of our lives and experience. The saying and doing are yet again constructed, or we might equally say creatively woven together in the context of human life.

Despite the creative power of the metaphor, it is not beyond criticism. I have tried to show that Juliet's rose metaphor is misleading because it underestimates the power of a name. Our critical faculties must keep a watch on our constructs, particularly if the constructed metaphor is apparently persuasive on first hearing. 'Reality' is not entirely a matter of our construction. Nevertheless, that persuasive ability in turn shows the metaphor's creative power.

5.2 Metaphors (ii): Ethics and Morals

Metaphors play a wide-ranging role in our language. I mention just one other example. Ethical and moral language is replete with metaphors:

Clean hands; pure heart; heart of gold; dirty hands/mind; conscience is clear; straight and narrow; salt of the earth; cutting corners; out in the open; doesn't know his right hand from his left; rotten to the core; leading astray; in your debt; I owe you; get even; make you pay for that; behaves like a cowboy; bury the hatchet; two wrongs don't make a right; out of the closet; don't demonise them; she's an angel; he thinks he's God.[84]

Let's briefly note a number of points with these ethics and moral metaphors.

I have tried to group the above metaphors by unifying motifs. For example, the first group is themed as 'purity' followed by spatial and then accounting metaphors. The last group draws on a spiritual realm. However, not everything fits neatly into a tidy group, for example, the strange quasi-arithmetic equation of wrongs not making a right uses standard ethics language but in an unusual or metaphorical way.

Perhaps the hatchet and cowboy metaphors are similarly a little unusual in the sense of not quite fitting with a group of similar themed metaphors. Or perhaps cowboys, indians and hatchets go together rather well. Theorising metaphorical structures into tidy groups which map onto other human practices can become somewhat strained.[85] Human life and practices provide endless scope for metaphors, including ethical ones.

As with Juliet's rose, these ethics metaphors may be used to express a truth about a person or their actions. They can also be used to distort and express outright falsehoods with convincing effect. That is again due to the power of those names incorporated into the metaphors.

Hence, the use of metaphors should not escape critical scrutiny. For example, if someone says 'he's gone off the straight and narrow', it may be wise to ask what he has done to merit the metaphor. The person may have done nothing reprehensible or foolish.

The metaphor's influence may be considerable, but its truth is not merely dependent on the metaphor itself. It should be related to the surrounding context and person or group to which it is applied. We may need to investigate the facts of this case.

---

[84] Some of these metaphors have biblical roots, as in Psalm 24:4: "The one who has clean hands and a pure heart, who does not trust in an idol or swear by a false god."

[85] I have based these brief comments on the work of George Lakoff (2004). His concern is with the cognitive influence of metaphors as a manifestation of neuro-linguistics, which is not a theme in this book.

Following on from the above, arguments which ride on such metaphors or closely related analogies should also be critically examined. Metaphors can 'take on a life of their own' and exert an influence which arises from the theme of this book—Adam names the animals.

Hence, the metaphorical effect should not be allowed a free ride and may need to be tested against the actual situation of which it purports to speak. A construct may come up against the ordered structure of creation—we would say it comes up against reality such as the facts of human behaviour. And again, the saying cannot be isolated from the doing within human life and God's ordered creation.

Juliet's rose is perhaps close to a moral metaphor which 'takes on a life of its own' but in a misleading way. However, a metaphor may simply give an illuminating emphasis or even become routine and unremarkable. Its effect and meaning are then subsumed into the overall linguistic context.

Metaphors may 'come to the end of their life' and 'die' by falling out of use; they become 'dead' metaphors. (Note these further 'life' themed metaphors.) That's part of the changeable nature of language, which goes along with changing perceptions in the wider culture.

Nevertheless, the point remains that metaphors can be powerful and persuasive like Juliet's rose, and are 'constructed' by ourselves to achieve their intended effect, which may be true or misleading and false.

In these ethical examples, the literal was frequently used to convey a reality from literal familiar experience to more abstract realities like love, ethics and morals. The rose did that very effectively, which made it all the more misleading, and so it may be with other ethical metaphors.

5.3 Metaphor or Reality? The Heart

Turning from deeper human concerns to physical objects and dying metaphors, we came across the heart previously when considering its function within the body.

Our contemporary use of 'function' can have a dual causal-teleological sense but within a material ontology, creating some tensions in the biological sciences. (3.1) We now return to the heart, this time from a metaphorical and construct perspective.

The heart is certainly a rich source of metaphors. Here is a sample:

Get to the heart of the matter; close to my heart; heartily agree with you; heartily sick of it/him/her; love you with all my heart; never far from my heart; bleeding heart; heart of gold; pour out my heart; hand on heart.

The reader can doubtless add many more to this list. In all these, the heart represents what is central to our being, particularly our emotional and even moral being. That is perhaps best expressed in the contrast of judging something by 'head or heart'—the rational versus the emotional.

We surely all recognise these heart metaphors as common metaphors where the implied significance of the heart is not to be taken literally. With the heart metaphor, we are drawing on past beliefs about role of the heart in human life which we no longer accept, though the metaphor lives on. We now know that the heart is merely a pump, which brings us down to earth with a bump. (Apologies for yet more metaphors!)

So, let's next consider the heart as a pump which pumps (literally) blood round the body. Before we had a developed biological understanding, the heart as the seat of our personality may have been at the literal end of people's understanding.[86] Then William Harvey discovered the circulation of the blood with the heart acting like a pump.

We now still have the heart as a metaphor for our emotional being while it is literally a pump. A pump cannot possibly substitute for the metaphorical sense of the seat of our emotional being, so that older view of the heart continues to give meaning to the metaphor we use extensively today. And again, it is we ourselves who construct this ongoing use.

But is the 'pump' itself a metaphor which has morphed into the literal reality? If we say the brain is a computer, the eye a camera, the cell is a machine, DNA is a code, and the mind is just neuron activity in the brain, we do not take these literally. Or do we?

Surely, DNA is a code and the heart really is a pump, though it is too much to say the cell is literally a machine or the eye is literally a camera, though there are similarities. And as for the mind being merely the activity of neurons in the brain—I say no more.[87]

---

[86] However, Hippocrates of Cos in *The Sacred Disease* seemed to recognise the role of the brain and the brain alone in our emotional life. (Hippocrates 1989, 175, XVII).

[87] What is the relation between mind and brain? Is the 'mind' merely a human construct detached from reality or is 'mind' more than neurons in the brain? (Dirckx 2019, 10).

We could run a similar set of questions around the teleological status of the heart being there *in order to* pump blood around the body. Does the function of the heart have both a causal and teleological sense or is the teleological merely a metaphor—for what?

The point is that we ourselves make these connections without precise definitions or criteria to set boundaries; there probably are no precise boundaries. Rather, something of ourselves within the lives we live enters the judgements we make, including metaphorical expressions. We judge the similarities and differences and thereby construct the metaphor.

That then becomes part of our understanding of the world, which shows a creative aspect that we named 'constructive', turning what might otherwise be a metaphorical pump into a real one with possibly, a real teleological sense to boot. Our perception of the heart's *purpose* is to pump.

Certainly, we make our pumps for a purpose. So, if the heart is a pump and is there in order to pump, where does that purpose come from? From an evolutionary process, which supposedly has no purpose? Perhaps the components of living systems are adapted 'in order to' survive. Or is purpose woven into the creation as is clear from the Genesis creation account? We will return to this point in due course, but for now I will draw our consideration of metaphors to a close.

Doubtless, there is much more to say about metaphors, related figurative language such as similes, analogies, metonymy and the many and varied ways they are used. However, our purpose is not to theorise, analyse or philosophise, but to show the important role these play in the wider creative power of language.

We have gone beyond Adam naming the animals. However, the constructive way in which we use metaphors is hopefully sufficient to show a continuity with the archetypal Adam naming the animals. Metaphors are rooted in our lives, work in different ways and are constructed to convey realities which are important to us.

They help us further order the world in line with our cultural mandate, though the complex subtlety of creation will not be perceived in the same way by everyone.

Sharon Dirckx argues that these are distinct. For the contrary view of the mind turning out to be the complex of brain functions see Patricia Smith Churchland (2002). Both argue that the answer to this question has profound implications for how we understand ourselves. In that respect at least, both agree and are correct.

We next look wider afield to two rather different examples of constructs where our judgements made in the context of our lives enter important practices of which language is a part.

5.4 Rule Constructs: Following a Rule—Addition '+2'

The next example is the simple arithmetical operation of addition. We would say that adding +1 is an arithmetic rule having a name—'addition'. We would also say that the result follows *necessarily* on applying the rule; it is a question of arithmetical logic where the result is necessarily true.

Our interest here is how the language of arithmetical logic is woven together with the practice of arithmetic and the social background where it arises and is applied. In particular, our judgements in part determine how arithmetic operates. Arithmetic logic is not something that stands entirely apart from ourselves and our judgements.

Now, we might readily accept that a complex mathematical proof requires great skill and creativity, but what might be so creative about simple addition? Besides which, the terms 'necessary', 'rule' and 'logic' do not leave much room for anything particularly creative apart from ingenuity within the scope of following the rules.

However, if we can see any creativity in a simple addition, that might be an example of a much wider human creativity. (We note in passing the new set of names describing mathematical practices.)

The philosopher Ludwig Wittgenstein considers what it means to apply a rule, here a rule of arithmetic. A student successfully carries out the addition '+1', and when reaching 1000 is told to continue with '+2'. The answers given by the student are 1000, 1004, 1008, at which point the teacher stops the student who is making an obvious mistake. But the student insists that their adding '+2' is the correct way to apply the rule for this addition.[88]

Of course, we all judge the teacher is correct, but why; what determines the *correct application of this rule,* and indeed of the rule-logic itself?

One such account is the metaphysics of Platonic forms or ideas, which I mention merely to illustrate a point. Plato's forms are supposedly independent of ourselves and reside in an unchanging realm of ideas. This seems to construe

[88] Wittgenstein 1997, 74e, §185.

mathematical 'necessity' quite well; there are logical rules that are outside ourselves, which we follow to get a true result.

Yet, we have no idea how to apply the Platonic forms to this case of even simple addition. How do the forms tell us whether the teacher or student is 'correct' because one adheres to the forms whereas the other does not? Hence, the forms tell us little about the necessary character of mathematical objects, properties or rules. Nor will any other metaphysical theory tell us anything, which is a frequent problem with such theories.[89]

So, perhaps it is by repetition and habit that one continues the *same rule* already carried out 1000 times, which is probably why Wittgenstein formulates the question in this way. Yet, the dispute is precisely about what the sense of this 'repetition' is in following the rule, and thereby what the sense of 'necessary', 'continue' the 'same rule' and indeed 'repeat' itself means.

Wittgenstein considers various interpretations where it might come as natural to the student to understand the addition and repetition determined by the rule in a different way.

Of course, not only does the teacher reject the student's interpretation, the teacher's interpretation is embedded in numerous practices holding in this society. The student will find life difficult if they insist on their interpretation, for example when paying bills.

A mistake can only take place within a shared arithmetical framework. The rule, or arithmetical logic, is shown in the context where the rule's necessary character is held in place by surrounding practices.

Here, Wittgenstein shows what it means to apply the rule as it is embedded in human practices. Following him, we have also emphasised the saying and doing woven together, starting with St Augustine learning the name of objects. In our example now, the numbers 'one', 'two', etc. do not name physical material objects like Augustine's chair. What these do refer to is harder to say. However,

---

[89] This position with respect to mathematics is not particularly that of Plato himself. It is derived from his theory of the Forms by later writers and is usually referred to as 'mathematical Platonism'. (Linnebo 2023) It may well be that mathematics can be brought down to logical principles as in Russell and Whitehead's *Principia Mathematica*. Mathematical creativity took these principles to remarkable conclusions, for example, with Kurt Gödel's Incompleteness Theorems. (Nagel & Newman, 1981). However, the same philosophical as opposed to logical question arises: why should we apply a mathematical rule in *this* way rather than in *that* way?

simple counting is applied to the apples in the fruit bowl, coins in payments and complex mathematics in scientific investigations.

We come again to the position where our judgements enter even the simplest of mathematical practices—addition. We devise the rules and practice them as rules for us to follow. Yet, these judgements are not detached from our wider society and human life, which takes place within a creation ordered by God.

While the student is constrained by the rules, the rules are not simply there as an eternally unchanging given; they arise from ourselves and are part of our constructive creativity: "*This* is how you add +2."

None of this is far-fetched. Looking more widely, Alex Bellos discusses how different peoples think about numbers. This may differ from our approach, though there are also similarities. Bellos concludes that given how different peoples understand numbers differently, our contemporary ability to represent numbers precisely with symbols is culturally constructed by ourselves. [90]

Bellos, like Wittgenstein, returns us to a constructive-creative role within wider social practices. Addition is not determined by a metaphysical abstraction but by human activity and judgements embedded in God's created order.

Yet in the process of such constructions, we produce the most remarkable mathematical systems and apply them in the sciences. The image of God thereby discerns something of the stunning order of creation in the application of advanced mathematics, and indeed in the mathematics itself. Again, our construction works within the order of creation and reveals something of that order, and perhaps even its beauty. Such is the dignity of ourselves as God's vice-regents and our cultural mandate to understand and rule.[91]

For the next example, given the remarkable congruence between mathematics and our scientific investigations of the world, we turn to that wider scientific investigation.

---

[90] For different ways of construing numbers by other cultures, see Alex Bellos, *Alex's Adventures in Numberland*, particularly his Chapter Zero (Bellos 2010, 13–41).

[91] Eugene Wigner, who won the Nobel Prize in Physics (1963), considered the application of mathematics to quantum theory and the wider natural sciences. He considers this near miraculous in his aptly titled paper *The Unreasonable Effectiveness of Mathematics in the Natural Sciences*. (Wigner 1960) He also mentions mathematical beauty and our creativity in his paper. His comments give more detail to a major theme of this book, though the possibility that mathematics, physics and our creativity might point to a transcendent divine origin is not considered by Wigner.

5.5 Explanatory Constructs: A Best Explanation

The natural sciences are often seen as the model of objective knowledge where we get away from personal and social influences and come, admittedly after much effort, to unprejudiced, objective, universally accepted and true conclusions. The question now is whether the sciences are good examples for a construct model of creativity.

What is known as the 'scientific method' involves a range of practices including observation, hypothesis and theory formation, experimental measurement and testing, theory confirmation, refutation or possibly theory adjustments along with mathematics and statistical methods. How precisely these are applied will depend on the different sciences and the problem being addressed.

Our concern here is not with technical details but to ask how, in a very general sense, we derive a conclusion from the detailed theories, experiments and research. It may sometimes be overwhelmingly obvious, but at other times much less so. We might even commit to a current theory despite anomalies. I will look at this in terms of science offering explanations and what might be the *best explanation.*[92]

To get a sense of what it is to be a good or best explanation and our role in judging this, I take a famous example from astronomy and related gravitational theory.

We expect scientific explanations to be formulated as testable theories. These should expose themselves to potential refutation by making testable predictions. This was famously emphasised by Karl Popper as a key part of the scientific method.

Yet, we cannot always know whether observed anomalies are due to an incorrect theory or undiscovered phenomena within that theory. Refutation is not always clear-cut.

For example, the planet Neptune was discovered by Adams and Leverrier in 1846 through calculations derived from anomalies in the orbit of Uranus. The scientists at the time remained with Newtonian gravitational theory and did not

---

[92] I will work with a rough and ready understanding of an 'explanation'. However, explanations for some outcome or result are many and varied including human motivations and interests, physical causes and processes, economic and social factors, they may be a somewhat vague guess, a hypothesis or a more substantial testable theory.

regard the anomalous orbit of Uranus as a refutation of Newton. Further investigation resolved the anomaly within the existing Newtonian theory. So, was Newtonian gravitational theory the final truth?

Anomalies in the orbit of Mercury also did not lead to a refutation of Newtonian gravitational theory. However, in this case, the anomaly was due to the shortcomings of Newtonian theory, which were remedied only later by Relativity Theory. The scientists of the day stayed with Newton for both cases and lived with the apparent anomaly in Mercury's orbit. That was their judgement of the *best explanation* available at the time.[93]

What might be a best explanation does not depend on one, but on various explanatory 'virtues'.[94] These are not precise criteria, but varied considerations informing scientific judgement. The virtues will have a differing weight depending on the particular case or science.

For example, the anomaly in the orbit of Mercury was not taken as a refutation of Newtonian theory because a best explanation will take into account the explanatory power of Newtonian theory and the absence of anything better. What might be 'better' is again judged by the virtues overall. Refutability is not everything, which was at a drawback to Popper's approach, important as it was.

Some of these virtues are fairly obvious. A theory should be fruitful in the sense of extending knowledge while maintaining its explanatory scope of existing knowledge, perhaps with an enhanced insight. That was the case with the increased explanatory scope of Relativity Theory and its deeper insight into the relation between space and time. Clearly there should also be no internal contradictions and ad-hoc arguments which circumvent difficulties.

Scientific explanations must deal with facts in the world which can be tested. In the case of the planets, Newtonian gravitational theory was an explanation dealing with the observed world. By contrast, the Genesis creation account is a functional one of divine agency in an ancient culture; it is not a scientific explanation of the material world.

---

93 Karl Popper's *Unended Quest* discusses the planets. (Popper 1980, 41–44)

94 I have taken the phrase 'virtues of a best explanation' from Peter Lipton. (Lipton 2004, 81, 121 ff.) Another good example is the Semmelweiss investigation into childbed fever in 1860. (Lipton 2004, 74 ff.) Lipton is a key text for best explanations. For some virtues of scientific best explanations see Bird (2003, 88–91). For an overview of scientific best explanations see Newton-Smith (1996, 226 ff.).

An explanation must also deal adequately with the relevant facts. For example, young earth creationism does not do so in the eyes of most scientist in the relevant disciplines.

As far as testing is concerned, in the physical sciences this will often involve predictions inferred from a theory. But a best explanation can employ other approaches. For example, Alister Mcgrath contrasts the importance of accommodation in evolutionary theory with prediction.[95] Perhaps however, we should not press this distinction too far since elements of prediction and accommodation are both present.

While the above are fairly obvious, other more subjective considerations may sometimes play a subsidiary role.

Simplicity is preferable to complexity when the latter adds nothing to the power of the explanation. The heliocentric explanation of planetary motion was 'simpler' than previous Ptolemaic system of epicycles.

Here however, more subjective considerations become prominent. For example, scientific theories are not always 'simple'. Relativity Theory is not obviously simpler than Newton's laws of gravity and motion. Nevertheless, scientists strive for simplicity which might include mathematical and conceptual elegance, perhaps even beauty.

These holistic considerations affect the larger scientific picture. For example, isolated anomalies are unlikely to change what is often called the scientific *paradigm*.[96] Current best explanations hold existing scientific theories in place, particularly when there is no better alternative available.

However, accumulating problems will loosen the current paradigm, making it more likely for something better to take over, where again, 'better' means theories formulated and judged within the overall virtues above.

While the virtues of a best explanation are not precise criteria, expert judgements are made by scientists within the state of scientific knowledge at the time. As Michael Polanyi argues in *Personal Knowledge*, they are also *personal* judgements within the scientific community.

While such judgements are 'objective' as to scientific method, they are not objective in the sense of being impersonally detached from the skill and

---

[95] McGrath 2009, 59–60.

[96] The classic work on scientific paradigms is Thomas Kuhn (1970), *The Structure of Scientific Revolutions*. For an online description of Kuhn's Paradigm Shift, see Bird 2002.

perspective of those making the judgements.[97] Those judgements enter into the application of the criteria above, and even in the selection of the criteria.

That personal element returns us to our constructive creativity as something of ourselves enters scientific practices through personal judgements which weigh what is the best explanation. Those personal judgements are not arbitrary or merely culture bound since they take place within God's ordered creation.

Hence, we speak of scientific knowledge transcending cultural differences due to the ordered creation within which we all live. And that also enables people from all cultures to participate in the scientific enterprise.

While this section is a huge simplification of a complex human endeavour, it is hopefully enough to show the creative way we construct and use our judgements, including the language of a best explanation, to understand God's order in creation. Again, the image of God is equipped to rule and carry out that cultural mandate.

5.6 Constructing Certainty: The Vanishing Shed

Despite our scientific knowledge and its technological applications, we might still have a nagging feeling that all this constructing of ours leaves little that is certain, even undermining the authority of scripture itself. So, I will use a final illustration of our linguistic constructing, which is a little different.

This example is deeply embedded in human life and our language while not being immediately obvious. It is also an example where philosophy can play a useful role in bringing to our attention what we rarely think about.

There is a saying that the only certainties in life are death and taxes. However, even in everyday experience, there may be more 'certainties' than just these two.

Isaac Bashevis Singer wrote a short story about a vanishing shed ('vanishing' as in ceasing to exist). Imagine the setting in a remote rural village where

---

[97] Michael Polanyi writes: "As human beings, we inevitably see the universe from a centre lying within ourselves and speak about it in terms of human language shaped by the exigencies of human intercourse. Any attempt rigorously to eliminate our human perspective from our picture of the world must lead to absurdity." Yet scientific knowledge is not confined to human opinion or subjectivity. For example, in the move from a Ptolemaic to Copernican system, he writes: "We have sound reasons for considering theoretical knowledge as more objective than immediate experience." (Polanyi 1974, 3–4) While 'more objective' also involves personal judgement, it is hard to deny objective truth and progress with the Copernican example.

someone's shed inexplicably vanishes. The locals were amazed, unsurprisingly. Fortunately the shed reappears in due course.[98]

This is an amusing story, but of course, sheds don't vanish in real life. Now, suppose you had a shed in your garden and one morning, it was gone. You report your loss to the police. The officer may have possible suspects in mind and proceeds to look for evidence to make an arrest and hopefully find your shed.

Imagine a suspect saying to the officer: "I deny stealing the shed. Have you thought of the possibility that it might just have vanished?" A truly novel defence! Yet, the suspect is probably right that the officer would not even have thought of the possibility of the shed simply vanishing. How does the officer even go about investigating whether the shed just vanished?

There are deeper philosophical implications to this apparently trivial if amusing story. Let's take another example, this one comes from Wittgenstein. His later work *On Certainty* deals with the certainties we consider in this section.

Among other examples he takes the mundane case of someone losing a book. Of course, the book hasn't just disappeared or vanished. There is no evidence for such things vanishing. But then strikingly, Wittgenstein notes it often happens that such a lost book is never found, raising the question why that should not be considered evidence of things just vanishing![99]

It is not only books which never turn up again, so do pens, rings, keys and a few years ago, a complete aeroplane disappeared off the coast of Australia. Why is this not *evidence* that things might just vanish?

To continue with the book, suppose I'm not sure whether I left the book in that drawer, so I check. This unremarkable practice where something is in doubt relies on something that is not in doubt, namely, that books don't just vanish. Now, suppose I doubted *that*, and the book wasn't in the drawer.

Going to check somewhere else would be pointless since I might have put it in the drawer and it subsequently vanished. But if I put it somewhere else and still couldn't find it, it may similarly have vanished! However, we will insist that the book *cannot* just have vanished, which is not based on evidence or arguments.

This certainty derives from the sense my life has. Without that certainty, my life starts to lose sense; why and where do I even begin looking for my book?

---

[98] Singer 1980, 62 ff. D.Z.Phillips reviews some philosophical questions arising from Zelig's shed, which first drew my attention to that particular example. (Phillips 1993, 171–192) This section is based on Wittgenstein's *On Certainty* (2006).

[99] Wittgenstein 2006, 19e, §134.

Doubt itself loses sense. Hence, the 'cannot' is a logical exclusion. It is not just an attitude which might and often does change, or differs from someone else's attitude. That certainly is woven into the fabric of my life if life is to make sense.

We can also say it is certain, and even true, that books and sheds don't just vanish. This is not some theory based on evidence about which we might be mistaken or where we need more evidence. While a philosopher may try to *justify* the book not vanishing, it seems mad to doubt it.

Indeed, since the philosopher's justification is arguable, it will not address the logical certainty that things don't just vanish. Hence, this logical certainty is not knowledge which may be mistaken, neither can it be justified by argument or evidence. [100]

Furthermore, it is not a question for the physical sciences to determine, since such logical certainties are embedded in scientific practices. If an experiment gives a different result, we don't just shrug and say "sometimes it's different."

We will look for changes in the conditions, the experiment itself or the theory on which it is based. There is an underlying conviction that we are dealing with an ordered world—the uniformity of nature. What that ordered uniformity *is*, is not a question for theorising but is shown in our scientific practices, as it is with the police officer investigating the vanishing shed.

We proceed on the belief of an ordered world, not one where "it's just different and sometimes things simply vanish." A different result for an experiment is not regarded as evidence that sometimes things work differently.

Notice how evidence, investigation, reasoning and argument turn around these logical certainties, which frame as it were, the way we reason. It makes no sense to doubt them, and so, following Wittgenstein, these logical certainties are sometimes called 'hinge beliefs'.[101]

---

[100] A good philosophical example was posed by Bertrand Russell. How do we know whether or not the universe, along with all our memories, came into existence five minutes ago? This is considered an epistemological question concerning our knowledge and might be used to encourage epistemological scepticism. A response based on the approach in the main text is that the universe coming into existence five minutes ago is logically excluded since it loses our bearing on human life. For example, if this were true, criminals in prison did not commit their crimes and should be released. The reader can work through other resultant absurdities.

[101] Wittgenstein 2006, 44e, §341. Danièle Moyal-Sharrock discusses and develops Wittgenstein's logical certainties or 'hinge' propositions. (Moyal-Sharrock 2007, 72–99)

Because of that logical *cannot*, we can investigate whether Fred stole the shed, and we can also doubt that he did so. However, if sheds might just vanish, it's hard to see how to make a case against Fred or anyone else; doubt itself loses its sense as we lose the contexts which make sense even of doubting.

The sense which our lives have turns as it were on such hinges; without that certainty, we lose our bearings on life.

We have come a long way from Juliet's rose metaphor, showing just a small part of the enormous variety in how the image of God interacts with and understands the creation. The use I have made of a 'construct' is not a tidy theoretical concept with neat sharp boundaries.

It reflects the riches of our language, to which I have hardly done justice. However, in all these cases, something of ourselves and our judgements enter into the way we use, or in this last case, don't use language. With hinge beliefs, though the words fit in with normal patterns of speaking, we do not accept statements about objects just vanishing, except in jokes and fictional stories.

Again, our linguistic practices are woven into human life. I have used the broad term 'construct', to show something of God's ordered creation.[102]

5.7 Linguistic Creativity Summary: Constructs and Reality

Let's summarise by drawing together the above very different examples of our linguistic creativity, along with some earlier points.

We recall that St Augustine relates how he learnt the names of objects as a child. This took place as he himself, along with his parents or elders, engaged in a learning *activity* where the doing and saying are woven together. This theme pervades the book, though in many different ways.

We considered the teleological function of the heart, house and home language, and functional-naming language with our artifacts. We went on to a biologist describing to me the taxonomy of living systems as being a 'construct'.

---

[102] I note in passing how Wittgenstein's thought opposes Descartes' *Cogito*: "I think therefore I am." (Descartes 1968, 53) By doubting everything he could possibly doubt, Descartes arrives at the certainty of the *Cogito*. Unfortunately, such systematic doubt loses the sense even of our language, where the Cogito itself no longer makes sense. What can the 'I' possibly *be* when swimming in a sea of doubt which loses the sense of our lives?

We have taken examples of the metaphors of Juliet's rose and ethics, metaphors which were close to being descriptions, an arithmetic rule-logic and the wider scientific method as a best explanation.

Finally, we looked at logical certainty and hinge beliefs. All of these involved us making judgements, which were woven together with our experience of human life as an individual and within a wider social and cultural context.

In the background was the archetypal Adam naming the animals.

These were all examples illustrating in very different ways the varied sense of the term 'construct'. My purpose was to show how varied are the ways we speak about things and how we bring something of ourselves to the way we speak which both reflects and also develops our understanding.

Yet, despite there being a constructive contribution from ourselves, these contexts are not wholly constructs of ours but part of the life we live. For example, the heart as a pump is part of our understanding of blood circulation and numerous related medical *practices*.

There is a bedrock reality which we cannot evade. A different construction of the heart may threaten those medical practices and so much else. Neither are such fundamental aspects of our lives all of the same kind.

We have a physical-pump, moral purity and emotional love. Mathematical rules and theorems are abstract logical systems which can represent physical realities but not the reality of love, ethics and values. That is part of the complex structure and richness of God's creation, which is not just about physical objects.

Hence, on the one hand, I have chosen the construct model to show that personal and the wider social creative aspect of our language use, and thereby also our understanding. We see God's creation through a perspective of ours where our language has a creative aspect illustrated by the archetype of Adam naming the animals. That is how the world 'really is' to the ANE and similarly for us, our world is in part seen through our constructs.

On the other hand, there is an important qualification; we are all under the same constraints within a world ordered by God, of which He is the Creator. That is particularly so when we look at material structures and processes. We then find that best explanations within scientific investigations lead to conclusions which apply to us all.

Some of our conclusions seem hard to believe, as with quantum physics. Sometimes, we must accept the provisional character of scientific knowledge, where there have been major changes or paradigm shifts in the past. Always, there seems more to discover where knowledge raises further questions. But other matters are surely beyond doubt; the planets go round the sun, the heart pumps blood round the body and sheds cannot just vanish!

All these considerations underlie a linguistic creativity in Adam naming the animals. He needs to carefully examine how these animals behave and how they are similar and different in their many ways, and what are the important differences.

That implicitly includes the material aspects, without which Adam cannot make the distinctions to name the animals. In doing this, he uses *his judgement* to determine what are relevant distinctions and similarities. And so, he names them and their kinds.

That starts to carry out the mandate to rule on God's behalf.

Our constructs interact with the reality of God's creation in many different ways. That may be for truth or falsehood, including moral and ethical issues which are part of God's ordered creation and not merely cultural constructs.

Yet within that ordered creation, there may also be legitimately different perspectives, such as that of the ANE with its functional ontology and our contemporary culture with a predominantly material ontology. We may be able to come to a richer point of view or we may need to learn more and correct our mistaken views of the creation.

Most importantly, there are the fundamental beliefs we hold about God and ourselves, which inform this book. The being and purposes of God, and also ourselves being in the image of God and having that cultural mandate, are not matters for us to construct.

These do not lie within Adam's domain to rule, but like so much else, require a proper context. That context for Christian believers is scripture, as it was for Christ himself.

6. Some Objections and Challenges

In this chapter, we look at some objections, along with what might be better described as challenges to my theme. Without making too much of the distinction, objections are most likely to come from believers themselves, whereas the challenges come from secular thought which all believers need to deal with.

To start with objections, some may arise from me being too uncritical about my application of the ancient Near East (ANE) on which I have relied.

Another objection is that I have done little detailed exegesis of the Hebrew text of Genesis, which might then have led me to different conclusions. These are certainly areas where much more could be done.

However, it was never my intention go beyond a limited scope on such matters since my focus was to develop my theme for human language from that ANE background to the Genesis creation account. More detailed discussions are available in the works I have referenced.

Nevertheless, there are further objections we need to look at, which arise from within, or are a consequence of, the ANE framework which I have accepted. The first three sections, which concern the three-tiered universe, are perhaps the most important because it puts pressure on the authority of scripture. This is not something we can just side-step by talking about Genesis describing how things appear to us (phenomena), or being metaphorical, poetry or some other familiar literary genre.

6.1 The Three-Tiered Universe (i): Functional and Material

Earlier, we noted that as Adam named the animals, there was an implicit hint in the text that he would take an increasing interest in the material aspect of creation. (4.1) This is because any effective naming must observe and understand the material aspects of animals to distinguish behaviours, physical forms and their relation to the environment.

After all, any functional order is expressed in the matter of creation. The material cannot be wholly eliminated from Adam's mandate to rule. Such a rule should not only reflect the purposes of God within the Genesis functional ontology, but must deal with all aspects of Adam's realm, including the material aspects. That is so, even if material features were not a matter of significant interest in the Genesis account or the wider ANE creation myths.

Such a latent material aspect to the text enabled us to complement the functional Genesis focus with a material understanding enriched by contemporary science, all of which is within the creation purposes of God. We called this a 'creation worldview' to move beyond function and material ontology terms while maintaining the Genesis functional emphasis within the prevalent perspective of the ANE.

Apart from Adam and the animals, it is surely the case that familiar everyday terms such as 'day', 'sky', 'land' 'seas' in the Genesis account also have a latent and familiar material sense in that they allow the same material possibilities and impose the same material constraints on people then as they do now.

But how far does that material sense intrude itself into the text? If a mistaken understanding is conveyed in the Genesis text, if only by a subsidiary material perspective, is the text itself mistaken?

One need hardly point out the possible theological implications, particularly to those who have a high view of scriptural authority. To fall back on the functional ontology of Genesis or stress its metaphorical character may get us out of this particular problem, but I want to take the more difficult route.

How do we deal with such an error in any material aspect of the text, even if it is not the focus of interest in the ANE? Can we still maintain the authority of the Genesis account? We must also keep a place for Adam's rule, the cultural mandate and our creative faculties, arising from the image of God.

That takes us to the three-tiered universe.

The Genesis account presents us with God creating the major structural features of our world, which He names. By the end of the third day, God has created and named 'day' and 'night'. He separated the waters above from the waters below by a partition, vault or firmament holding up the waters above, which is named ‘sky’. Finally, we have the further creation order of ‘land’ and ‘seas’ which are named. (Gen. 1:1–10)

We have seen how this is all within a divine function-purpose ontology. (2.5) More functions follow with the vegetation, the lights set in the firmament above. Then the living creatures and finally, the man and woman who are to procreate and rule, being in the image of God; that is their function.

With many aspects of the Genesis creation account, the functional does not need any further material supplement. For example, if the days of creation are best seen in relation to temple inauguration, that conveys the *function* of a temple rather than its material construction or contemporary cosmology.

The interpretation then leads towards the presence of God with people, as would be the case with a temple. We have seen that the temple significance in the creation account is a garden in a creation made by God for us to dwell in alongside His presence. Hence again, the functional emphasis of Genesis within the ANE.

The theological importance of the cosmos as a temple where God dwells with us cannot be adequately expressed by a quasi-scientific material ontology.[103]

Nevertheless, in the ANE as well as the Genesis account, there is a broadly shared background which has significant material implications. John Hilber summarises:

> “While metaphorical and theologically symbolic language was used by the ancients to convey their belief systems, certain shared assumptions are discernible from the iconographical and textual evidence: (1) a three-tiered universe with a physical, underworld realm; (2) an earth-sun system wherein the sun moved around a flat earth that is fixed in relation to a body of

[103] Walton summarises the creation account as a cosmic temple inauguration: “Setting up its functions for the benefit of humanity, with God dwelling in relationship with his creatures.” (Walton 2009, 162. See also Walton 2015, 100 ff.) Wenham, perhaps, is a little weak here: “Maybe a daily chat between the Almighty and his people was customary.” (Wenham 1987, 76) Better is: “God conversed with the first man in a visible shape, as the Father and Instructor of His children. This human mode of intercourse between man and God is not a mere figure of speech, but a reality.” (Keil and Delitzsch 1975, 97)

subterranean water; (3) an extension of cosmic waters (a reservoir) beyond the atmosphere into the heavenly realm."[104]

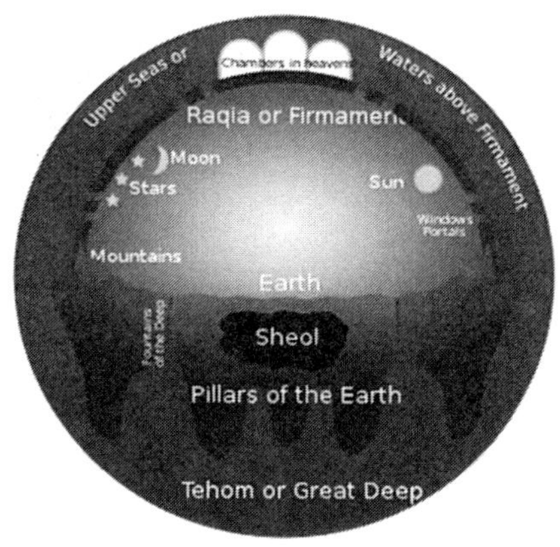

The accompanying diagram of a three-tiered universe illustrates how this cosmic geography might look.[105] There is an upper sea of cosmic water kept in place by a solid partition or firmament of some sort. The heavenly bodies are set into the base of this firmament with further waters beneath the earth.

Hilber notes that some of this cosmic geography was common with people throughout the world, particularly the solid partition or firmament positioned over the flat earth disk surrounded or possibly floating on water.

That there should be a cosmic ocean above the firmament is less common.[106] However, it was present in Mesopotamia and Egypt, where the Enuma Elish is the best-known account as Marduk's first act of creation is to split the body of the slain goddess Tiamat, separating the two severed parts at the end of Tablet IV.[107]

We might speculate how such a belief arose. People look up at the blue sky from which the rain, sometimes heavy, comes. Clearly, the blue above is a watery canopy of oceanic proportion. The clouds are windows into those waters up there, which must be held up by some kind of barrier or quasi-solid firmament or partition.

Then it seems logical that the heavenly bodies are set into this firmament. Yes, these *functioned* to govern day and night and they serve as signs to mark sacred times and days and years, which is the point made in the Genesis text.

---

[104] Hilber 2020, 82. Walton calls this the 'cosmic geography'. He shows how this cosmic geography was an understanding in both Genesis and other ANE creation accounts. (Walton 2018, 131 ff.). More technical detail is in Wayne Horowitz (2011).

[105] The three-tiered universe is by an Unknown Author licensed under Creative Commons CC BY-SA.

[106] Hilber 2020, 53–54. He conducts of critical discussion of various scholarly views pp. 53–57.

[107] Hilber 2020, 69. Also Dalley 2008, 255.

However, that is not merely how the world functioned as a cosmic temple in the lives of these ancient people, but also how it appeared as structured on an observational appearance to the senses.[108]

One criticism we can make of these contemporary pictorial models is that they reflect our own material ontology, which is unsurprising since we produce the diagrams from our contemporary perspective. They exhibit a material structure, which is a reinterpretation by us of aspects of the ANE understanding.

However, this fails to represent the close relation between the material and the divine, where the ANE did not make any such sharp distinction.

A better example is in the accompanying diagram from Egypt.[109]

The sky goddess Nut embeds the stars on her body. The air god Shu maintains the separation between Nut and the earth god Geb. The sun god Amun-Re sails his barque over the heavenly waters above Nut. Osiris is the god of the underworld shown partly emerged from his domain. The gods are integral to the structure of creation.

Following a critical discussion of various scholarly positions, Hilber fairly notes the tendency to read ancient texts in too literal a way. That certainly seems the case with contemporary sketches of the ancient cosmology. The details of that ancient cosmology were also often unclear or inconsistent. But then Hilber continues:

> "There are good reasons to expect, *a priori*, that the ancients did construct mental models of their cosmos and these ideas would follow cognitions that are common to other pre-scientific peoples. Also, some ancient notions of cosmic geography were not *just* phenomenological or analogical, but were also false perception of the material world."[110]

---

[108] The way things appear to the senses is often called a 'phenomenal' appearance. This terminology follows Emmanuel Kant who made the distinction between how things appear to us as 'phenomena' due to the way our senses and understanding are structured, and how things are in themselves, or 'noumena'. (Kant 1996, 205 ff. A235/B294)

[109] Illustration of the Egyptian sky goddess Nut and other deities by an Unknown Author licensed under Creative Commons CC BY-SA.

[110] Hilber 2020, 57–58.

It is this false perception of physical reality which we must deal with since it seems to intrude itself into the Genesis creation account with possible echoes elsewhere.

Hilber turns our attention to Israel's shared cosmic assumptions across a range of scriptural references. He notes of the ancient geocentric model with possibly a flat earth, that it may have had some practical uses, but such models were not merely phenomenal in the sense of how things appear to us from our vantage point. They were false in their physical aspect.[111]

Regarding the Genesis creation account, an important element named by God is the separation of water above the vault or firmament from the water under the firmament. (Gen. 1:6–8) Hilber discusses this at length, noting that a good case can be made that this is metaphorical language.

However, his conclusion after further analysis and textual exegesis is that the ANE view, shared by Genesis, was of a cosmic ocean above.[112] And I would add, it is God who names where He cannot be mistaken, rather than Adam who might be mistaken.

It may be easier to go along with a functional or even a metaphorical interpretation and thereby side-step the awkward implication that the text is mistaken. However, we will take the more difficult route and say that we now know the text is mistaken in so far as it reflects the beliefs of the time about the cosmic geography.

That is the problem which we must address if we are to maintain the authority of scripture in the case of the Genesis creation account.

6.2 The Three-Tiered Universe (ii): Tomatoes and Divine Accommodation

In this section, we will adopt the approach that God accommodates His revelation in scripture, at least in some respects, to the limitation of human knowledge and the cultural understanding of the time. This is nothing new and Hilber gives an extensive overview of examples of this accommodation approach in church history.[113]

---

[111] Hilber 2020, 74. By 'operational', Hilber refers to practical uses. See also Hilber's footnote 127 pp. 74–75.

[112] Hilber 2020, 82. We first noted the cosmic ocean in the Shamash tablet. (2.6).

[113] Hilber 2020, 84 ff.

Hilber's own approach is a linguistic one based on contemporary Relevance Theory. In brief, our everyday communication works with explicit and implicit meanings within the shared background assumptions that speakers hold. Hence, the relevant sense of what is being said and heard is conveyed with much being left unsaid, since it lies in that shared background context.

Communication is thereby simplified and made much more efficient, though misunderstanding may creep in more readily. The everyday illustrations which Hilber gives are particularly suited to our theme. However, I will not deal with Relevance Theory but instead use an example from Hilber, which is a good instance of accommodation and illustrates Relevance Theory from everyday life. I will then apply this to the Genesis account.

The example also helps us appreciate that accommodating the understanding of others is a familiar practice of our own. Hence, if God gives His revelation through human language into human cultures, it is reasonable to suppose He accommodates some aspects of the cultural understanding, just as we do.[114] I will also consider the theological and scriptural justification for taking this position.

Consider going to your local greengrocer to buy some tomatoes. On your left as you enter the store is the fruit and on your right are the vegetables. There is plenty of choice and you are in a hurry. Do you head towards the apples, oranges and bananas on the left or towards the potatoes, leeks and onions on the right to find your tomatoes? Probably towards the right since the tomatoes are usually located with the vegetables. They certainly are in my local greengrocer.

However, did you know that tomatoes are a fruit? And if so, why are they among the vegetables?[115]

A number of further questions now arise: (i) Are the customers being misled as to what a tomato is, biologically? (ii) If the storekeeper knows that tomatoes are biological fruit, why is the location of the tomatoes not moved from the vegetables to the fruit section? Is the storekeeper now guilty of a deliberate deception? (iii) Why doesn't a government standards officer insist that the tomatoes are displayed together with the fruit, which is their correct biological category? This is surely easy enough to do.

---

[114] Hilber 2020, 139.

[115] Tomatoes are not the only fruit usually placed with the vegetables, so are courgettes. I do not intend to biologically distinguish fruit from vegetables; the point is that the shop accommodates the expectations of the customers given their purpose for using the shop.

We will address these questions from the contextual perspective which is simply a part of everyday life.

We first note that the function or purpose of the greengrocer is to sell a product to customers and to help those customers reach and select their products efficiently. This means the store will work with the expectations of the customers. If those customers expect to find the tomatoes with the vegetables, the store will place them there. Doing so helps the store to function effectively and keeps the customers happy.

Put differently, it is not the store's *function* or purpose to educate customers in biology. That can be done elsewhere. For example, suppose the store co-operates with a local school to set up a biology display. Such a display might then place tomatoes with fruit and indicate why the tomato is classed as a fruit since education is now the functional purpose of the display.

To continue with the store, is anyone being deceived? If so, is that an intentional deception on the part of those who know the tomato's correct biological classification and can to do something about it?

Again, Hilber rightly points us to the context. While this is not an immediate linguistic context but a practical one of where tomatoes are placed in a grocery store, the placement is also part of a linguistic context.

A customer might ask: "Where are the tomatoes?"

The reply might be: "Over on your right next to the potatoes."

Or an assistant might ask: "Where do you want these tomatoes?"

The storekeeper might reply: "They are always on the right with the vegetables; just put them next to the potatoes."

The practices of the greengrocer work with the, usually unarticulated, assumptions of the customer. Those practices then elicit a relevant behaviour, which enables the customer to efficiently get what they are looking for. This is a major theme of Relevance Theory where Hilber shows with examples how even everyday speaking works within a context of implicit but understood assumptions to efficiently convey meaning.

Hence, whether the storekeeper is biologically ignorant or well-informed, what is relevant to questions of truth and deception are the customer expectations in this context of the store's function and the customer's needs.

"Is it true that tomatoes are fruit and not vegetables?"

This question is determined by biology and established educational processes, not by the function of the shop. Hence biology is not an adequate reason to govern where they are placed in the shop.

In summary, we might say that the storekeeper accommodates customer expectations relevant to the store's function and customer needs, without being concerned to implement other truths about tomatoes. Whatever customers might believe about tomatoes, including having no view on the fruit/vegetable question or having never even considered it, the store is deceiving no one.

It is right to add that questions of truth can quite properly be raised. Perhaps the tomatoes are of inferior quality while being priced at a premium level, all this known to the shopkeeper but not the customer. Instead of being corrected, the customer's assumptions and ignorance are then exploited. This now becomes an ethical issue, which was not the case when merely placing the tomatoes with the vegetables.

Indeed, tomatoes and all the other goods can be positioned in many different ways, none of which is deceptive. Why should the products not be placed in order of individual size or by the colour spectrum? This is not deceiving anyone but is again likely to frustrate customers even more than putting the tomatoes with the fruit.[116]

Let's now turn to the ANE and the Genesis creation account and see whether the tomato analogy can help.

I accept the longstanding position that God is the author of scripture while His revelation is given to us in human language. Hence, the study of the original languages and a careful contextual exegesis of the text is vital. However, the text and its language also lie within a wider culture, and we have seen how the Genesis text shares something of the ANE background, which must also be considered.

In Genesis, we most likely have a three-tiered universe which is focussed on the purposeful functional ontology of the components of creation. However, it is not wholly disconnected from a material-structural understanding.

---

[116] Hilber illustrates *Relevance Theory* with contemporary linguistic examples. A good case is the office conversation where he analyses the implicit contextual background assumptions to make sense of what is explicitly stated. It nicely shows how we ourselves use an implicit shared contextual background to economise what is actually explicitly stated. (Hilber 2020, 128 ff.)

In the wider ANE, the creation was also intimately related to various gods. That is not the case with Genesis where God is wholly distinct from His creation. Nevertheless, in so far as Genesis has a shared ANE structural aspect, to some degree the text reflects a mistaken structural understanding.

Applying our analogy and the purpose of the grocery store, we should ask for the purpose of the Genesis text. This is surely to convey God as the Creator, His relation to creation and ourselves and the varied functional purposes of what is created. Such was the default understanding of the Israelites which strongly contradicts the beliefs of the surrounding peoples.

Of course, we should not press the analogy too far. While there was a major cultural conflict embedded in the Genesis text, and intentionally so, that is hardly the case at the greengrocer! What is fair about the analogy is that Genesis, like the shop, had a clear purpose while also, like the shop, leaving some matters in abeyance. In the case of the shop, it was the biological status of the tomatoes; in the case of Genesis, it was the accuracy of the created structures in the text.

Certainly, God is not ignorant about the ordered structure of creation, whether functional or material. After all, He made it. Rather, He accommodated the Genesis revelation to the understanding of the time. But that raises a further question; why should God accommodate that understanding rather than correct it? Surely, it would not be too difficult to convey the work of creation in broad outline as we know it to be.

Yet, we should hesitate before asking that God's revelation in scripture is formed by truth in all its material details. If we imagine ourselves in the pre-Copernican age of say the fourteenth century, we would be most surprised to find a later and very different cosmology coming our way.

Quite likely, we would not even believe it, and we would certainly not understand why it was so. Scepticism about the accuracy of the text will then be repeated until at last a generation sees that they have the truth. And will that be our generation or are there further shifts to come even in our scientific understanding? All of which will undermine what is important for us to know as opposed to being subject to the contingencies of human knowledge.

However, I want to address any scepticism towards accommodation in the Genesis account by the theme of this book, which is itself a scriptural theme.

As we noted previously, God honours our cultural mandate. It requires us to investigate and frequently, to correct initial impressions. Revelation does not override this except in so far as it concerns those matters vital to our relation with

God, where these are not a matter of investigation, scientific development or cultural constructs. That is not the domain of Adam's rule.

Continuing with the three-tiered universe, some believers may take an apparent error in the text of the Genesis creation account to conflict with inerrancy and verbal inspiration.

But suppose we ask how we should apply inerrancy and inspired verbal truth when the text itself is causing problems for our interpretation of inerrancy in this case? The scriptural text is not there merely to confirm our views but to challenge and deepen them—even on inerrancy.

Let's return to Adam's rule in his domain. That rule implies we need to investigate and understand God's creation, at least to an extent which makes our rule effective. Hence Adam naming the animals. However, surely there is no guarantee that Adam's early understanding or that of the wider ANE is correct.

The same applies to what the original authors/compilers of the text might have thought about the universe's structure. Adam and we ourselves may need to be corrected and humbled by the subtle complexity of creation. That is all part of the unfolding of our cultural mandate.

This is conveyed by the text as it faithfully records Adam's and the wider ANE's faulty understanding of creation's structure conveyed in the text itself. That faulty understanding continued for several millennia even to current times, where we ourselves may still be significantly corrected in our scientific knowledge.

Hence, we need not have an error in the text, rather, the text strikingly conveys the fallibility of human knowledge in what is Adam's domain to investigate, understand and rule. It also conveys God accommodating His revelation to human understanding in so far as it applies to Adam's domain; his rule and responsibility is honoured and upheld by God rather than being overridden in a way that Adam was in no position to understand.

However, regardless of the ANE's understanding of the universe's structure, the Genesis message is that God is its creator. Surely no one can be in doubt on that point.

Finally, our view of inerrancy and verbal inspiration should be subordinate to scripture itself. With respect to the three-tiered universe, the intended inerrancy teaches us that human knowledge, including our own scientific investigation, is limited and fallible, as it was for Adam and the ANE.

So, I close this section by returning to our cultural mandate, which arises from the functional ontology of the Genesis creation and the image of God. Accepting the focus on a functional ontology of the creation account, there is nevertheless a latent material aspect to that functional ontology.

This was implicit in Adam naming the animals and more obvious in the structure of the three-tiered universe. The latter was a widely held ANE understanding and was wrong in a structural sense. That mistaken understanding cannot be salvaged by appealing to the functional ontology of the ANE.

While the functional comes through clearly and is the primary focus of interest, the functional is expressed in a material world which we experience. Function cannot be wholly divorced from matter and hence, the Genesis understanding of that material aspect is partly a mistaken structural one.

However, that need not undermine the inerrancy of scripture if we remember the cultural mandate. When Adam names, this is partly to understand something of God's creation so that he and those who follow him might rule. The mandate does not mean he gets it right merely from quick superficial observation, and neither did the rest of the human race for several millennia.

God does not override our mandate as vice-regents by spoon-feeding us as to the causal-structure of creation. We need to do the hard work and exercise the necessary self-criticism.

That God accommodates His revelation to human cultures, its presuppositions and understanding is not only a theological matter of our mandate as vice-regents. Accommodation is pervasive in our own speaking and practices, which is the theme of Relevance Theory illustrated by the tomatoes.

Contextual assumptions are also pervasive in our wider culture, some of which we may challenge even while we are embedded in that culture. This should help us understand why God might do likewise as He spoke through human authors into that ancient world.

As a result, those ancient Israelites were focussed on what mattered most and opposed beliefs about the divine which were false. Those Israelites would not be distracted by the subtlety and complexity of creation which they could not understand and would likely reject. That understanding would only come as we carry out our cultural mandate.

As we discover more of the subtle complexity of creation, we will be amazed. Whether that brings us to worship the Creator rather than the creation is another matter to which we will turn in the next chapter.

6.3 Is Genesis Mistaken? Language, Framing Questions and Relativism

To close the worry about Genesis being mistaken in its cosmic geography, I want to again draw attention to the constructive-creative power of our language. Since that construction is carried out by ourselves within a surrounding culture, we will also consider the related implications of cultural relativism.

To start, how we pose the question of the Genesis creation text being mistaken has a significant effect on the subsequent discussion.

Suppose someone asks:

> "What is the plain meaning of the text? Surely we need to discern its literal meaning since it is describing the process of creation. What does the text actually say? Are you really telling me that Genesis is mistaken!"

Terms like 'plain meaning', 'literal', 'describing the process', 'actually say', 'really telling me', 'Genesis is mistaken' are expressions which readily lead to a particular kind of discussion. The question embeds some of our material, scientifically formed cultural assumptions.

A phrase like 'describing the process of creation' will be understood in material-causal terms governing the apparent plain and literal meaning of the text. Even if the questioner believes in a young earth and rejects scientific views on cosmological developments and evolution, that material ontology is still operative in the presuppositions underlying the terms of the question.

Furthermore, terms like 'plain meaning' have a rhetorical effect in suggesting that the obvious is being denied.

It is hard to resist the thrust of the question, but also a good illustration of the power of our language and the way we construct meaning. So, let's continue with our linguistic abilities and rephrase or re-construct the question in a different direction.

> "What was the purpose of the text in its original context? What were the beliefs of those ancient peoples about the gods and the creation itself? How would *you* relate a creation account if your hearers were likely to reject your views of creation, and as a likely consequence, undermining anything else you said about God as well? For an important example, how might a missionary relate the Genesis account to a pre-scientific society?"

The point here is not to enter debates about whether the overwhelming scientific consensus is right or wrong. It has often been wrong in the past, though it does not follow that a young earth view is an improvement any more than the ancient three-tiered universe is an improvement.

The point is to note the power of language even in posing questions. That power is also apparent from Relevance Theory applied to our own language when what we say relies on or 'accommodates' a whole range of shared assumptions. Even terms like 'inerrant' and 'infallible' can take on a life of their own.

It is part of my response that scripture should control these terms and the way we pose and answer questions. While it is fine to explore any question that is asked, subsequent discussion should bring to light hidden assumptions and the worldviews which are in play.

That includes the way these are used to frame questions. Our approach should also have theological integrity that in the Genesis case, rests on our mandate as God's vice-regents, which is a mandate God honours. Hence, the ancient but mistaken cosmology is accommodated by God with those ancient peoples and generations of subsequent ones.

There is a further possible objection to language being creative in a constructive sense. It seems that concerns about ultimate truths and significance fall back onto our linguistic creativity, which may then confine us to the beliefs and practices of different cultures.

Out constructs are now human perspectives which are said to be *relative* to particular cultures. The contextual emphasis of this book seems to play into the hands of relativists who claim that we cannot transcend such perspectives to achieve an objective viewpoint. That is, a viewpoint which is true regardless of the beliefs of individuals, societies or cultures.[117]

Pontius Pilate would have approved in his famous question: "What is truth?" (John 18:38). That question still echoes down the ages.

---

[117] 'Relativism' comes in various forms which deny claims to objective truth; we cannot get beyond a human or cultural perspective. Relativism may be applied to different areas such as ethics and morality, claims to objective knowledge (epistemology) and more sweeping denials of there being ultimate objective truths. In the main text, we are concerned with ultimate claims about purpose and human significance. An online overview is in Baghramian and Carter (2022).

While some secular thinkers adopt a relativist stance, believers may also be concerned that the theme of this book plays into the relativist narrative. We have a contextual emphasis leading to a three-tiered cosmos, which was widely held in the ANE, and was present in Genesis itself.

This cosmic model is a good example of a cultural construct which we know to be mistaken. Consequently, doubt is thrown onto the rest of the Genesis account. That account concerns ultimate origins, purpose and human significance, with ultimate beliefs precisely where the relativists aim their criticism.

The case for relativism, especially concerning religious beliefs about ultimate truth, is not confined to a creative-constructive aspect with language. The mere fact of different belief systems, differences within them and some views excluded as heresies, suggests all such beliefs are mere opinion sustained by dominant and usually oppressive power structures.

There is nothing objective which adjudicates between these different viewpoints. However, I am not concerned with detailed arguments and will stay within my theme. The response to this objection is that any linguistic creativity and constructing on our part does not take place in a vacuum.

While literature allows the imagination to run free, even then words must retain much of their familiar meaning to be comprehensible. That meaning starts in childhood as the doing and saying are woven together, which we saw with St Augustine. In the case of the sciences, there is certainly much creativity in theory formation, mathematical application and testing.

However, all this takes place within a world which we share within the same physical possibilities and constraints. Hence, the sciences have a consensus on knowledge in many areas. With the archetypal Adam, we have seen that this world is our domain to rule with the Genesis account of considerable influence in scientific developments as well as social improvements. We certainly know much more about cosmology that the ANE ever did.

Hence, there is much which resists a relativist perspective, but perhaps relativism has its greatest influence on questions of significance and value.

Here we come to the heart of the matter, which is the significance of humanity and ultimate truths about the world. The relativist is concerned to see off claims where that Genesis account tells us about ultimate truth and human significance. However, these are not within Adam's domain to rule or construct.

Hence, Genesis sets itself firmly against all contrary belief systems, just as it did against pagan beliefs in ancient times. Genesis also opposes the relativist perspective. One may not believe, but what is the relativist's alternative on ultimate truth, value, human significance and dignity?

We end up in a world with no ultimate purpose and no particular significance to human life. There is no basis for human dignity and value. In any case, life on Earth will probably end before too long and be lost in the epochs leading to the final heat death of the universe.

And ironically, this bleak outlook is then undermined as relativism itself is just another belief system relative to the passing foibles of particular cultures. Nevertheless, the relativist claims to hold an objective truth that all other ultimate truths are culture bound, itself being the exception. This is hardly convincing.[118]

By contrast, it is the Genesis account which addresses the human condition and our longing for significance, purpose, dignity and so much else. It does so without skirting around the uglier realities of human life and societies.

So, leaving aside further apologetic details, there is good reason why a believer should embrace the full implications of the image of God, including our constructive-linguistic creativity.

6.4 The Primordial State—Created 'Ex-nihilo'?

Another objection which arises from our approach to the Genesis context in the ANE concerns that original non-ordered state of creation. This is not a question about integrating our scientific knowledge or familiar use of language with Genesis. It is the way we interpret the Genesis text on the ultimate origin of that initial state of dark, watery non-order.

What was prior to the initial undifferentiated non-ordered primordial state of darkness and water? As we see the scheme of separation, function and naming lead to an increasingly ordered creation, what was that initial state separated *from*?

If it was not separated from anything, or created from nothing, 'ex-nihilo', it seems that initial primordial state was itself eternal. And if the initial state was separated from something else, was that something else perhaps eternal? When

---

[118] There have been many philosophical attempts to find some basis for ethics, values, human dignity and rights by non-transcendent means. An overview is in Spencer 2016, 125 ff. See also section 6.5 for some further examples.

God created the heavens and the earth, did He also create that initial state or did He merely set to work on an already present primordial state?[119]

However, to ask this question assumes a material ontology; it makes sense to ask what was there prior to that dark unordered watery beginning. Were those waters always there or were they created 'ex-nihilo'? The waters are familiar material water. By contrast, if we think about a functional ontology and then ask what the state was prior to any order, the answer would be that there was no order. The waters now represent an absence of functional differentiation.

Then if the question is pressed further to what that non-order is like, we again get the answer of darkness and water. The question cannot be taken any further if the focus is on function, which would be the case with a Genesis functional ontology. Non-order as darkness and water is as far back as it makes sense to go with a functional ontology.

Walton summarises this as follows:

> "A function-orientated ontology/cosmology bypasses the questions that modern scholars often ask of the ancient world: Did they have a concept of 'creation out of nothing'? These questions have significance only in a material ontology. If creation is not viewed as concerned with the physical making of things, these questions cannot be approached through the texts."[120]

Suppose we next position ourselves in what I previously called a creational worldview, which accommodates a material aspect to the creation within the divine-functional ontology of the Genesis creation account. From a scientific point of view, we cannot go to a state prior to the 'Big Bang'.

Neither can science take us to any divine intention. Equally with the Genesis account to ask what was there prior to the imposition of order, that question cannot be answered from the functional account of Genesis. We are simply given that initial state of non-order as understood in the ANE, with no sensible answer to the question how that non-order arose.

---

[119] In Plato's *Timaeus,* the 'demiurge' is the supreme craftsman or creator who does not create from nothing, but brings order from non-ordered matter. (Plato 1977, 41–43, §29–31; 72, §53) In his commentary, Desmond Lee notes the limitations of the divine purpose in the creative process. (Plato 1977, 96)

[120] Walton 2018, 151.

However, suppose we narrow our attention to the text itself and the interpretation of the Hebrew terms within a wider scriptural use.

The question now centres on the translation of the first clause, "In the beginning God created the heavens and the earth." How does that relate to the creative work of God which follows? Unsurprisingly, there are various scholarly views on this, and it is not the purpose of this book to enter those debates. I merely note the following.

Gordon Wenham considers four different interpretations and discusses them in detail.[121] He concludes: "It is therefore quite feasible for a mention of the initial act of creation (v1) to be followed by an account of the ordering of the different parts of the universe (vv2–31)."[122]

If Genesis 1:1 is that initial act of creation, we then need not go any further back to question what was there prior to the ordering of what was created. God created the initial non-order which he then proceeds to order. Wenham deals with the Hebrew terms and constructions, which we will not consider further beyond the following observation.

Since there are differing interpretations which Wenham considers, we may have to accept that the text alone may not be conclusive. However, if we keep the divine-functional ontology of the Genesis creation account in mind, we have a coherent interpretation which cannot take us to anything prior to the initial non-ordered state; the text does not address what that was separated from.[123]

This ambiguity might frustrate us when we want answers to our questions. We tend to think in yes/no terms, these being the only acceptable logical alternatives. We then ask whether the primordial state was eternally existent or

---

[121] Wenham 1987, 11 ff.

[122] Wenham 1987, 15. Wenham summarises his preferred interpretation as the last of four which he considers. He summarises Gen 1 as: "A main clause describing the first act of creation. Vv 2 and 3 describe subsequent phases of God's creative activity." (Ibid. 11) Walton also discusses this question and comes to a similar conclusion though by somewhat different arguments. (Walton 2015a, 123–127) Walton places more weight on his functional ontology understanding of Genesis, which then fits well with his interpretation. John Hilber considers three possible options and comes to a similar conclusion, with a particular focus on Relevance Theory. (Hilber 2020, 175–181)

[123] That does not exclude other passages presenting or implying an 'ex-nihilo' creation, as well as paying more attention to the material aspect of creation. See Hilber for a Relevance Theory approach. (Hilber 2020, 175–181)

not; did God bring it into existence 'ex-nihilo' or did He not. However, the text may not be concerned to address the question which we ask, neither need it be confined to yes/no answers as we might wish.

Nevertheless, if not in Genesis, we can conclude from elsewhere that whatever there was, materially or functionally, God created it. For example:

> "For in Him all things were created: things in heaven and on earth, visible and invisible, whether thrones or powers or rulers or authorities; all things have been created through Him and for Him." (Col.1:16)[124]

Here is the ultimate origin, whether of matter, functions or that initial functional non-order.

6.5 Various Challenges: The Deconstruction of Reality

In this section, we leave the ANE behind and turn to our contemporary society with what might be better described as challenges rather than objections to our theme. A believer might 'object' to the way I have approached the Genesis creation account with reasoned criticism, as above.

By contrast, in this section we look at some de-constructions of reality which all believers and others must address, regardless of their views on the significance of the ANE or my constructive-creative theme.

Hence, the term 'challenge', which arises from our own surrounding cultural trends rather than believers' 'objections' to the theme of this book. These challenges often arise from wider philosophical claims and arguments.

To deal with such challenges I do not propose to abandon our creative linguistic constructing, which then diminishes the image of God in ourselves and will not address the challenges we face. Instead, any constructing needs to take place within a scriptural-creation context, where we will now see what happens when that divine-transcendent context is lost.

Put differently and to use our previous term, when a 'creation worldview' is lost and replaced by a secular, atheistic or materialist worldview, this will affect how people and societies *construct* their understanding of the world and ourselves, particularly with respect to questions of ultimate truth, value and

---

124 Also Ps. 148.5; Prov. 28:22–27.

significance. We will also see that a new worldview is at work with, ironically, metaphysical tendencies and a striking internal incoherence.

In this section, we consider three different examples having a linguistic-constructive emphasis. This potentially affects our understanding of human values and significance. I start with a philosophical move in the way language produces meaning. We then go on to wider issues.

Example 1: Philosophy, Logic and Language

This first example is a philosophical move, which attempts to identify a necessary principle for our language to make sense.

During the twentieth century, language took a more central role in what is usually called the 'linguistic turn'. Different approaches to philosophical problems had largely failed to reach firm and agreed conclusions, so it seemed that a philosophical study of language might resolve at least some longstanding questions. Yet, potentially destructive tendencies were also at work.

The underlying problem was that any philosophy seeking access to some truth or reality outside ourselves and our faculties, which was a classic metaphysical question, had lost credibility for many philosophers.

One approach was to find some principle which was grounded in an objective reality, rather than built on beliefs, opinions, emotions, metaphysical theories or other matters of dubious and disputable worth.

A significant development in the linguistic turn was *logical positivism*. Given the apparent dead-end of metaphysical theories, this new direction sought to confine linguistic meaning to what was verifiable in familiar experience or the sciences, along with reasoning based on sound logical principles.

Here, so it was thought, was a firm foundation to knowledge.

However, this marginalised many important questions concerning God, ethics and the big stories of human significance, purpose and value as pseudo-questions. These were not knowledge in the sense or being verifiable as true or false determined by investigation or scientific theory and experiment, and hence they could not be construed as even being true or false.

Rather, they were considered as expressions of emotion, or instances of 'emotivism' for short. Some went further and considered such questions, particularly metaphysical questions, as meaningless.

The big stories of human significance and value are called 'metanarratives', and the loss of these will likely be serious. If the image of God is lost, which is part of a metanarrative and not amenable to empirical investigation, where does it leave the significance, value and dignity of ourselves as human beings?[125]

A.J. Ayer is a good example, with the so-called verification principle. Any sentence is 'factually significant' if it can be verified by experience such as observation, other methods employed by the sciences or what follows logically from these. If this cannot be done, we are not dealing with a genuine or meaningful statement. That would be the case with moral assertions using terms such as 'ought', which are not making statements about verifiable facts.

Ayer also notes that a sentence may be emotionally significant without being literally significant. Religious and ethical belief may be about emotions and feeling, but such beliefs do not express, as philosophers would say, genuine propositions which might be true or false in a sense not merely confined to our beliefs and opinions.[126]

What might be the problem with this bold and radical philosophical move? To repeat an earlier example, suppose we ask whether there is a God or a foundation to ethics beyond ourselves and our beliefs, to which we ought to conform our lives.

Let's suppose this asks a pseudo-question which is not a genuine question in the sense above, because it is beyond verification as true or false by science, experience or being a question of logic. But that is to make an implicit metaphysical judgement.

For example, the possible working of God in the world is a metaphysical (as well as a theological) question. If it is eliminated by the verification principle, that principle then privileges itself to judge what we can know about a divine perspective governing the nature of our world and the flow of history, which implies a metaphysical perspective. To judge a metaphysical question is to adopt a metaphysical perspective.

---

[125] Logical Positivism is not the only destructive linguistic approach. Several decades later, Jean-François Lyotard writes from a perspective which has moved beyond optimistic social progress where knowledge is dependent on metanarratives, religions and much philosophy being examples. This led to a 'postmodern' condition. "Simplifying in the extreme, I define *postmodern* as an incredulity to metanarratives." (Lyotard 1997, xxiv) He goes on to mention the crisis in metaphysics brought about by the sciences. While Lyotard later had regrets about this particular book, scepticism towards metanarratives is ongoing, though often with a metanarrative of its own.

[126] Ayer 1990, 16–17.

There was also an internal contradiction. Logical Positivism was itself beyond verification in experience or by science, neither was it a merely a logical claim. While insisting that meaningful statements and genuine questions should conform to these conditions, logical positivism itself did not do so.

How ironic that logic positivism should be undermined by logic itself at its own foundations. On the other hand, if such a principle was to be sustained it would have to lie outside logic itself, which would again show its metaphysical character.

To construe meaningful language on what is given in experience or deduced from experience and science might initially seem firmly grounded in reality. However, the outcome was logical incoherence and self-defeating, hence this movement was of limited influence.

One need not believe, but a religious, scriptural context is quite capable of making sense of matters which are not in the domain of science. As for everyday experience and evidence, we have the testimony of eye-witnesses in the Gospels, again providing a proper context for religious beliefs.

Logical positivism shows an approach to constructing knowledge by applying a philosophical principle to determine what is meaningful language and what are genuine questions.

Certainly ingenious and constructively creative, but also a dead-end.

Example 2: Reconstructing Knowledge—Science and Society

In this and the following example, we look at two more important contemporary trends which share an ideological character. An *ideology* is a set of ideas going beyond historical or scientific data and knowledge. An ideology has a sweeping view of human life and history through an overriding idea which becomes the controlling perspective or logos of reasoning.

An ideology may rightly identify aspects of our lives, societies and cultures which are good or evil. However, its purpose is not to come to a balanced and limited assessment to explain some aspects of the human condition; the overriding purpose is to change it. The results have too often been tragic.[127]

---

[127] The words in the main text echo what Karl Marx wrote, and which are inscribed on his gravestone. "The philosophers have only interpreted the world, in various ways. The point, however, is to change it." This is Thesis 11 in his Theses on Feuerbach (1845).

If logical positivism expected to get some of its verification from the sciences, we have to think again. Might science itself become shifting sand?

We have seen Michael Polanyi argue in *Personal Knowledge* that scientific judgements are also *personal* judgements within the scientific community. (5.5) While such judgements are 'objective' as to scientific method, they are not objective in the sense of being impersonally detached from the skill and perspective of those making the judgements.

The point of scientific knowledge being *personal* is not merely the obvious one that it is scientists who examine causes, structures and reach best explanations by experiments, research and judgements embedded in their individual and collective expertise.

They exercise a creative aspect of human language where we saw an example with teleological language in the biological sciences. (3.1) We also see that creativity in the names we give to some extremely strange physical quantum phenomena, again with Adam and the animals as the archetype.

We can go beyond Polanyi in that it is not just *personal* knowledge but the image of God, which shows itself in scientists as human persons and God's vice-regents. But for the moment, we will leave this scriptural and theological perspective aside and see what might then happen.

Turning to the personal side of scientific judgements, we now ask *how* these are made in their personal and wider social aspect. For this, we turn to the social study of science since such judgments are made in an interpersonal social environment.

Jonathan Potter poses the question, and first does so with a traditional view of science in mind:

> "How is science organised as a social institution in such a way that scientists regularly and successfully produce objective facts? And conversely, what distorting social factors may result in the production of scientific errors?"[128]

Potter develops the point that this traditional approach assumes that scientists are concerned to come to 'objective facts' in their research practices. Successful

[128] Potter 1997,17.

or true scientific theories and knowledge are grounded on careful investigation of the facts which constitute that objective reality.

I note that this reflects something of Polanyi's comment earlier about an objective as well as personal-social dimension to research. Such objectivity makes it likely that social research into scientific practices shows how competent scientific practice is conducted in its social aspect. This is reinforced if we accept that it is important to know how the wider social ethos supports or undermines good scientific practices. That ethos is likely to have at least some influence.

However, a danger of the traditional view is that it may constrain the scope of social studies to clarifying the scientific method and good practice. Errors in scientific conclusions are assigned to defective methods and poor practice arising from the social background. Potter makes this point and is rightly concerned if the social study of science should be biased or constrained in this way.

I accept that the influence of social factors on scientific practices are many and varied, all of which should be open to study. While it is valuable to know how the social context may help or hinder good scientific practices, it is not always clear whether or to what extent good practices are implemented. Sometimes it is a mixed bag, complex and hard to judge. Hence, pre-judging social practices by what are supposedly examples of good science leading to objective results may limit or skew such social research.

Potter is rightly concerned that social research might be subordinated to the traditional view of science. We should recognise that the social ethos can influence and may oppose scientific investigation in many ways. That includes social research having its own ideologically motivated agenda or inbuilt bias.[129]

For example, there are contemporary ideological trends in some social sciences (and academic humanities departments). Much of this comes under the

---

[129] Potter goes on to survey contemporary ideological trends in the social research of scientific practices, with examples from some of the leading players. (Potter 1997, 17–41) He also shows how linguistic rhetoric is used in the production and construction of 'objective facts', for example, the depersonalised discourse in science research papers such as the familiar phrase 'the evidence/data shows that'. (Ibid. 151, ff.) However, we must remember that such rhetoric may describe actual realities, which Potter acknowledges, though that is not his emphasis. (Ibid. 139)
Historically, the Galileo affair is a good example of an interaction of personalities, a still limited astronomical science and the external culture, particularly the church and its theological context. An overview is in McMullin 2019, 51–64.

heading of 'Critical Theory' which sees the social order built on structures of power, interest and oppression. We briefly note some of these elsewhere.

Therefore ironically, even the social study of science may itself be influenced by such pressures which no longer notice their own defects as they also align with a new ideology. Hence the wider social ethos can act in many ways to distort scientific practices and even the social research itself, regardless of one's stance towards the traditional view of science.

All of this should be critically scrutinised.

Contemporary trends can also exploit philosophical problems with the traditional view of science. For example, there is the age-old metaphysical problem: how to move from scientific theory and conclusions to true knowledge of objective reality. There are related philosophical problems with terms such as 'reality', 'objective' and 'truth'.

If these are all questionable, it may be that scientific practices are not about knowledge of reality but again, the interests of dominant powers. Hence, there are a number of reasons why we should at least consider approaches which avoid prior assumptions about objective scientific facts and knowledge. Potter does so as he sets out a more radical 'constructionist' approach with examples from some of its significant advocates.[130]

Given the theme of this book, any 'construction' of scientific knowledge is of interest. Where contemporary social and academic trends see established social structures as oppressive to disadvantaged groups, one might interpret even a scientific consensus as arising from self-interest. What is counted as 'knowledge' mirrors social structures of power and control. Inevitably then, individuals, academic and commercial organisations conducting social research into scientific practices have interests of their own.[131]

And so, Potter rightly notes that much of this more radical social research in different ways builds narratives of its own; this line of research is uncritically part of the social environment being investigated. He gives a small example

---

[130] Potter 1997, 34 ff. For a striking critique of the absurdities of some contemporary philosophical positions which question the foundations of scientific knowledge see Sokal and Bricmont (1999). This may then influence and be influenced by the wider social context which ties any social research into that same wider ethos.

[131] Potter gives some examples, though not the particular trends which I will briefly illustrate. (Potter 1997, 27, 38)

affecting his own analysis.[132] It then looks somewhat like other self-referencing and self-defeating positions we come across in this section (6.5).

We can even say that it embeds its own metaphysical assumptions. For example, to replace what is in part a metaphysical perspective of 'truth' and 'objective reality' is to make a metaphysical judgement and thereby adopt a metaphysical position.

Even so, we should consider the possibility that there is more to this radical interpretation in the sociology of science which should not be prematurely dismissed. It may on occasions play a role. Such a more radical approach has certainly freed itself from subordination to the traditional model of science!

Let's then suppose powerful social movements exploit the social aspect of science within a larger changing social ethos to de-construct or re-construct knowledge for their own ends. There may be changes to what is considered a human good along with changes in knowledge more widely. For example:

> "Challenging oppressive race, class and gender relations in society requires a reconstruction of knowledge so that we have some basis from which to change these damaging and dehumanising systems of oppression."[133]

What is considered 'knowledge' is now closely connected with more 'positive' values, which starts to change the sense of 'knowledge'.

Some of this may be desirable, some less so. The premise is that 'knowledge', including scientific knowledge, too readily reflects oppressive systems. For example, what was previously considered a fact as to one's biological sex is now reconstructed as more fluid and subordinate to a person's sense of gender, at least according to some. A traditional but supposedly oppressive social gender stereotype is thereby reconstructed.

Hence, some suppose that a trans-woman, who is a biological male, is nevertheless a woman and should therefore have access to women's spaces and

---

[132] Potter 1997, 34.

[133] Andersen & Hill Collins 1995, 4. Their anthology concerns the United States. Much of this may be true and ensuring such groups are heard makes it possible to reduce social inequity. Less clear is what any reconstructed knowledge should be, since what is considered 'knowledge' by some particular group may be less acceptable to others. What will constrain a new privileged group pursuing their interests and determining acceptable knowledge by oppressive means? Indeed, what might 'knowledge' even mean?

participate in women's sports. As well as practical consequences, there are clearly scientific implications along with a display of the creative power of language in a reconstruction of knowledge and personal identities.

What is less clear is how the resulting reconstruction grounds its own notions of 'good', 'equality' and 'justice'; what is just and good for some may be a new form of oppression to others. These are values lying outside any science, but given the *sociology* of science, values will be incorporated into any reconstruction of knowledge within a social environment.

What wins out in the end may not be determined by science but by the most powerful interests. That includes any reconstructions of knowledge on more radical social lines driven by a further set of interests implemented by oppressing others. For example, if we are to shift power from one group to another, it makes little sense to give free speech equally to all.

The new powers need to corner the language of virtue since language itself plays a powerful role in existing systems of privilege and oppression. That seems an entirely plausible outcome if we are the originators and arbiters of our constructs.

Such trends affect contemporary Western cultures and are causing serious problems within churches. It is then again tempting to reject any 'constructing' when it comes to our understanding and the creative power of language, which is the theme of this book.

However, such a rejection may also compromise the scope of the image of God, so how do deal with this objection without compromising the constructive perspective of this book or scripture itself?

We should first acknowledge that there are many instances which, to a greater or lesser degree, illustrate the more radical view about wider social influences on the sciences. This is unsurprising since the sciences are also human practices incorporating a personal-social dimension as Polanyi noted earlier.

Some religious beliefs and practices will also fall under this radical view as human constructs built on social and cultural foundations. We might think that some structures of church government or the priesthood have more to do with power and interest rather than scripture or the priesthood of all believers.

Secular and atheist systems claiming to improve the lot of humanity can equally become structures of oppression covered in the language of virtue and freedom. Doubtless, there is much to say about this, but I will confine my comments to the theme of this book.

While accepting the above, an important point is that no science, and that includes the sociology of science, can answer the question of God's being and existence, what is the foundation of values and ethics, whether human beings have any ultimate significance and value, or if there is any purpose to the ordered structure of our material ontology.

That is not part of Adam's domain to rule, and hence such questions are outside the content of scientific knowledge, whether reconstructed or not.

Certainly, the creation, including scientific knowledge, gives us a sense of the being of God which we then suppress. (Rom 1:18 ff.) However, God's being and existence is not the subject of scientific investigation, the solution of mathematical equations or statistical social and opinion surveys.

Hence, in challenging oppressive race, class and gender relations, there is no way to determine what these should or ought to be apart from the predominant ethos of a particular society. There is nothing transcending any society which a social ethos ought to follow as determined by any science.

Similarly, we lose the image of God along with the divine dignity as a basis for human values. If a society allows slavery, as has been the predominant throughout human history, who is to say that is 'wrong' or 'unjust'? Why should the beliefs and practices of our society challenge oppressive race, class and gender relations elsewhere?[134]

The physical and related sciences, which seem the most impervious to personal or social prejudice and pressure, are also vulnerable. We briefly noted this earlier with the effect of gender identities on women's rights overriding biological considerations. These sciences rest on a prior belief that there is an ordered structure to the world, which we can investigate and understand.

This might be a belief held by some societies at various times, as it has been with our own and fits well with a creation worldview. That will then most likely

---

[134] We have come across a similar point previously with the example of FGM and St Augustine absorbing social language and practices from childhood. (2.1) However, the image of God can also recognise better practices. Sharon James describes some of the value related changes which the Christian faith brought to many parts of the world. (James 2021) Sometimes, a culture can and ought to export higher human aspirations elsewhere. Nick Spencer makes a similar case with a greater but realistic emphasis on the complexity, difficulties and opposition encountered along the way. (Spencer 2016)

lead to the position which Potter initially put to us, that the facts themselves determine truth. It will also play an important role in inspiring scientific investigations into a creation ordered by God.

However, if such a belief is a product of the dominant social ethos which will differ between cultures and societies, we are less likely to see the physical sciences as showing something of the structure and order of the material world. The assumptions built into the social research may aid and abet this.

What is the position we have taken in this book? We have not simply adopted Potter's more objective position on scientific knowledge. Rather, within a scriptural context, God has created the world with an ordered structure, which is a material structure imbued with non-material aspects such as purpose and value showing us something of the Creator's eternal power and divine nature (Rom. 1:20).

Significance, value and a witness to the being of God are woven into the creation. We ourselves are similarly material beings while in the image of God. Hence, the linguistic-constructive activity on our part takes place within that ordered creation and our cultural mandate to rule—for good or evil. There is room for constructive creativity on our part, but the sciences and many mundane activities must work within that order.

Finally, as noted in other cases, this more radical social interpretation of the sciences de-constructs itself; it is internally incoherent. If social interests determine scientific knowledge, then such interests will also construct this radical interpretation itself while at the same time making it dependent on a new set of predominant social interests.

There can be no further claim to any overarching 'truth' beyond the truths of the predominant powers, which are themselves socially and linguistically constructed.

In summary, the result of this scriptural worldview is that both the value-beliefs and the material-structural beliefs have led to enormous benefits, often with science and value working in tandem. One need only think of medical practices and wider health reforms.

By contrast, the loss of the scriptural view will likely lose or pervert human dignity and value as well as any sense of a true and ordered creation, and the sciences which presuppose such an order.

Again, there is a linguistic creativity, but with ourselves constructing new realities. However, there is also an incoherence which continues as we look more widely beyond the sciences.

Example 3: Literature—Power, Interest and Oppression

To close with a final challenge, we turn more explicitly to the creative power of language, powerful enough to construct a new reality. Equally, the following is a convenient summary of previous challenges, as well as the relativist position which we included in the section on objections (6.3).

For at least some philosophers and many in academic humanities and social science departments, language is now seen as a vehicle by which powerful groups control the structures of societies to serve their own interests. There is no final ultimate 'truth' against which we can evaluate social trends and beliefs.

What we therefore need to do is 'deconstruct' the surface meaning of a written text or verbal communication since the meaning of words is unstable. Such a deconstruction exposes the underlying rhetoric as it serves interests of power by the linguistic manipulation of weaker groups. That applies to any metanarrative 'truths' as well.

To take an example, Steven Cohan and Linda Shires illustrate this wider philosophical conclusion as they apply linguistic theory to narrative fiction.[135] They discuss how a reader may identify the theme "man and/or his relation to the universe, where the expectations of a work's universal significance, metaphysical coherence, and thematic unity define an agenda for reading which has political and social implications in what it excludes as well as includes."

---

[135] In the background of their approach is Ferdinand de Saussure (1857–1913), who had a significant influence on linguistic theory. In his exposition of Saussure, David Holdcroft opens with the heart of Saussure's view, the socially constructed aspect of language as an arbitrary system of signs. The meaning of these signs is derived from their position within the linguistic system. (Holdcroft 1991, i) Saussure also distinguishes between the 'sign' as the word or sound and the 'signified', the idea or concept. How our doing woven together with the saying gives a sense to the sign, is much less clear. Saussure's key concepts are in Saussure 1966, 66, 117, 120.
The significance and study of signs is part of semiotics, which is another aspect of human creativity. Saussure was one of its founders, though I will not take semiotics further. See also Potter 1997, 68 ff.

In their example, a universalising notion of 'man' may suppress "issues of culture, race, class, and gender that question the western, white, patriarchal and bourgeois conception of 'man' as a synonym for 'human'."[136]

Certainly, all too often language is used to such ends. Given our theme on the creative power of human language, this is a potentially serious matter affecting how we construe good and evil along with justice, equality and human dignity. These worthy value-names can go in many directions.

We might think of state propaganda or statements and arguments from political parties, spin doctors, conspiracy theorists and pressure groups. Religious believers and church organisations are not free from this where biblical, theological and other virtue language is distorted to yield novel meanings. Extreme cases are sects or cults.

Ironically, those most committed to exposing and deconstructing established structures of power and interest also try to propagate and thereby privilege some 'truth' of their own. They explain this in lectures and books without expecting these to be deconstructed!

I noted earlier that we will try to locate language within the larger purpose of human life. What such a purpose might be is important to most of us, but it is not a question to be resolved by everyday experience or any science. Analysing language exclusively as a means of manipulation to maintain power and interests also seems inadequate, though at times that needs to be done.

Wider metaphysical theories might initially appeal, but there is no consensus on how these get us to reality, truth or knowledge. While we need not deny that all the above might have something important to say, we are unlikely to get definitive answers from such directions.

In summary, there are consequences to abandoning what we have called a creation worldview and associated transcendent realities. We have incoherent new truths along with an associated reality which often have a metaphysical character while denying the validity of any ultimate truth.

Rather than rejecting a constructive aspect to human understanding, believers need to recognise that there is a conflict between belief systems or worldviews where our linguistic constructions may be for truth or falsehood, good or evil. The image can and should recognise and correct what is wrong and

[136] Cohan and Shires 1997, 24.

unjust, including where these are embedded in social structures, which I have acknowledged. However, without the transcendent foundations of the image in God's creation, we will simply introduce new distortions which disfigure and disorder God's creation, including ourselves.

But why should that be? Can anything more be said about good, evil and the distortions we might introduce? To address this important question and its implications for us, we turn to the next chapter and continue with Genesis and the ANE.

7. What is Creation's 'Good'?

The Genesis creation account is not only about God ordering the creation from that initial state of non-order in a functional ontology. God also saw that His work was 'good', indeed on completion, God saw that His work was 'very good'.[137]

The question here is what might be the sense of 'good' in the first chapter of Genesis, and how that sense relates to ourselves. We should not be surprised to find a functional sense of 'good' in the Genesis account. There may also be a further sense to 'good' beyond a functional good, and we need to consider if and how it relates to the creation account.

As before, we will try to connect that ancient Near East (ANE) to our own contemporary understanding of 'good', which has varied but also inter-related meanings.

Since our Western culture has been influenced by the ancient Greeks, we start by relating our contemporary use of the term 'good' to the approach of one of their leading philosophers. A cultural heritage can go back a long way; how we speak and think does not always arise from our own more recent wisdom. Rather, it is likely part of our common humanity, which is also present in the Genesis creation account.

As we proceed, we should not lose sight of our constructive-linguistic theme. We are using the term 'good' across related contexts which give it varied but inter-related meanings. Our constructive speaking is embedded in and makes sense of human life. However, in the application to God, the sense of 'good' will be determined by the Genesis account rather than by any constructions of ours.

---

[137] Genesis 1:3, 10, 12, 18, 21. 25, 31.

7.1 Varied 'Goods' in Aristotelian and Contemporary Use

There is nothing new in describing a piece of work or activity of ours as 'good'. This goes back at least as far as Aristotle, who makes some important points which resonate with our own use of the term.

Aristotle opens his *Nicomachean Ethics* with:

> "Every art, and every science reduced to a teachable form, and in like manner every action and moral choice, aims, it is thought, at some good: for which reason a common and by no means a bad description of the Chief Good is, 'that which all things aim at' … Again, since actions and arts and sciences are many, the Ends likewise come to be many: of the healing art, for instance, health; of the ship-building art, a vessel; of the military art, victory; and of domestic management, wealth; are respectively the Ends."[138]

Important ends like health, victory and wealth require subsidiary activities, which are subordinate 'goods' to the superior ends or 'goods' to which those activities contribute. For example, artisan manufacture such as making bridles or other parts of a horse's trappings are the skills of horsemanship.

This is an example of activities which are subordinate and contribute to higher ends for which we need to ride and control the horse. Hence, there is a hierarchy of means and ends in human endeavours which all seek some good.

For Aristotle, these varied goods were to achieve 'the Chief Good' as 'that at which all things aim at'.[139]

Good as Functional

We should immediately notice the teleological orientation of Aristotle's thought in relation to human activity, including the things we make and manufacture—our artefacts. These all have ends which very often contribute to further ends.

We can equally say we make things for a purpose by giving them a function, which is why we make them. We previously saw that our use of the term

---

[138] Aristotle 2005, Bk.1:1.

[139] I shall use the short and commonly used phrase 'final good' to emphasise the teleological or 'final' goal or end that the many actions and goods aim at.

'function' can be analysed as having a causal component, what something does or causes to happen, and a teleological component, which is the purpose for which we make it. (3.1) When we introduced the ANE understanding of 'existence', we noted this with the amusing cartoon of the invention of the wheel. (3.2)

We can now take a step further and say that if the function is achieved, that is characterised as 'good'. Here the sense of good is, in the first instance, concerned with something functioning as intended to achieve its end, purpose or goal.

In the case of our artefacts, that goal is intended by ourselves. Equally, that goal may well contribute to further goals which are, hopefully, also good in that functional sense.

This is surely familiar territory. Suppose we enjoy cycling and purchase a new e-bike. Its battery powered motor is intended to help us up hills, go further or gives that extra boost when we are tired. Assuming it does the job, we say the purchase was a good decision and the bike itself is 'really good'.

The functional effectiveness of the e-bike really is 'good' in that it does what was intended. The e-bike may give us additional pleasure in the process, for example, requiring less effort on our part, again experienced as an intended 'good'. There may be multiple functional goods which are achieved.

But we need not stop there. The e-bike may help us achieve further ends which would otherwise not be achieved, or not achieved so efficiently. If we can now reach a destination more quickly, or perhaps the destination was previously beyond our range, that then enables us to accomplish something else, again achieving further functional goods. And so on.

We can speak of 'good' as functional in that dual causal and purposeful goal-directed sense, which we will call or name a *functional good.*

Good as Relational and Ethical

We next ask whether the term 'good' means anything more than 'to function as intended' along with a sense of approval of successful functioning. Unless there is a significant connection with human values, the use of 'good' with our artifacts will be limited.

And of course, there are connections with human values.

Continuing first with Aristotle, all these ends aim at a chief or final good. But before considering this ultimate goal, we should note that Aristotle ranges much more widely than the goals or teleological functions of our artefacts. He also considers human behaviours such as the exercise of moral virtues and various ways these might apply.

His examples are courage, temperance or self-control, desires or appetites, liberality, magnanimity, attitudes towards anger, social virtues of amiability and friendship, concern with truth and falsehood, modesty and a variety of intellectual virtues. The opposite of many of these are also considered. A particularly important virtue is justice, which Aristotle considers in various aspects.

The artefacts we make may be involved and connected with achieving many of these moral virtues. We need only think of medical practices. Hence, 'good' is not merely about functioning effectively in some efficient or material-causal sense, but may also be about achieving ethical goals or ends, particularly where this concerns our own activities and behaviours.[140]

As with our artefacts, while Aristotle's thought on the moral virtues is wide-ranging, it is hardly news to us. We would readily describe these ethical characteristics as good, and call a person who practiced them as good.

Furthermore, we know that neither the things we make, how we use them, nor our accompanying behaviours are always good in this ethical sense. Aristotle also writes about the many ways we fail to achieve the good and do the opposite; we might think here of the contrast between nuclear medical applications, nuclear power generation and nuclear weapons.[141]

We should further note that the ethical is closely connected to how we *relate* to others by helping or harming them. So, we might equally say that an ethical good in many ways overlaps with a relational good.

What we have then is a widening vision of how our artefacts *and* our actions and behaviours contribute to a chief or final good. There is a complex and varied ethical-relational dimension as well as a material-causal-functional one, all with a teleological orientation. Hence, we can speak of 'good' as ethical and relational; we will call or name this an *ethical good* and a *relational good*.

---

[140] Aristotle 2005, Bk. III-VI.

[141] On occasions we may pursue a good end but by means which cannot be described as 'good' in an ethical or relational sense. For example, in war it may be a functional and ethical 'good' that a wicked enemy is defeated, but killing enemy soldiers and the inevitable civilian deaths may not be a 'good' in an ethical sense. Evaluating some of these 'goods' may be complex and ambiguous.

But what is that ultimate, chief or final good?

A Final Good as Human Happiness or Flourishing

For Aristotle, the final good was human happiness, which we should not confuse with many kinds of passing pleasures. This good includes but also goes beyond the utility-good of artisan or manufacturing skills. Many virtues are exercised to achieve some other end, but that is not the case with happiness.[142]

Achieving happiness seems to be for its own sake, not as a means to something else. We might call it an unconditional good; it is not itself a condition for something else.

Aristotle's philosophy had a teleological orientation where the potential might become actual, which also applies to human nature. He thereby subsumes manufactured *and* ethical/virtue goods under 'the chief good', which is to attain the teleological potential of our nature rather than something else beyond that.[143]

Here, we might be more hesitant for follow him. While we are unlikely to deny the importance of happiness, is Aristotle's rather elevated sense adequate? For example, a Christian believer is more likely to say that holiness or Christ-likeness is the highest good in this life.

When asked which commandment was the greatest, Jesus replied: "To love the Lord your God with all your heart and with all your soul and with all your mind." The second was: 'Love your neighbour as yourself'. (Matt. 22:37–38)

If these were the greatest commandments, we might conclude that in obeying these we would find our ultimate good with happiness not always immediately present; this ultimate good might be costly.

Furthermore, 'happiness' may not always be accompanied by the best motives and may be merely self-centred at the expense of others, though of course, that would conflict with justice and other virtues. So, perhaps Aristotle had a somewhat more abstract sense of that final good and of happiness.

---

[142] Aristotle 1976, 73–74, Bk. 1: vii. Also 326 ff., Bk. 10:vi-viii. Aristotle's term for this happiness was 'eudaimonia' where 'eu' translates as good and 'daimon' as spirit or life. For an online overview, see Kraut (2022).

Aristotle was not the first to give this important place to happiness. Socrates also considered happiness as being an end in itself rather than a means to something else. It is an unconditional good dependent on wisdom for our good use of other things. See the *Euthydemus*. (Plato 2021)

[143] Aristotle 1976, 86–87, Bk. 1:xii.

Despite misgivings, both Christian and much secular thought may well accept Aristotle's position, particularly if it is rephrased in terms such as human flourishing, well-being or even blessedness, to use a religious term.

Despite the pain and effort required to achieve this, human flourishing is surely an end that ought to be pursued. However, how we conceive and achieve such flourishing is another matter.

We can show this varied sense of 'good' in a simple example. Suppose someone says: "I told the truth but it didn't do anyone any good."

Let's assume that someone was told that a planned course of action would fail with serious consequences. That would be a functional not-good if those consequences were not intended. There is also an ethical context of telling the truth, and presumably on this occasion the good of truth-telling is to achieve further good ends or at least avoid a 'not-good' end. However, the immediate purpose (functional outcome) for telling the truth was not achieved and the well-being, flourishing or happiness of various parties was frustrated. A relational good may also have been damaged in the process.

These different goods are bound together in contexts of human life and relations, which are all reflected in our language, as with this trivial example. Even so, in telling the truth for the benefit of others, that person was seeking a greater or final good, which has at least an echo of Aristotle's happiness.

Hence, we can speak of many goods aiming for some ultimate goal or state; we will call or name this a *final good*. We might even go so far as to speak of *the* final good.

Good as Pristine Perfection

A further sense of 'good' is that of pristine perfection which cannot be bettered. This sense is rarely used of our artefacts since what we make invariably requires compromises. Our e-bike earlier must consider the price, the weight of the bike and of the battery, the materials used, different ways of designing the suspension, ease of repair, the availability of spares and so on. Different customers will prefer a somewhat different compromise.

Compromise is built into the product and arises from the very nature of the created order. For example, the ecosystem on planet Earth is maintained by many causal processes and structures which need to function together in a balanced way. We may call this an overall good but not a pristine perfection. We would be hard put to imagine what that would be like or how it would be maintained.

Hence, the sense of something being a 'pristine good' has little application though one might apply it to some final good to which all other goods contribute. Unfortunately, that is beyond our experience.

But when it comes to what God *is* and what He does, we might be reluctant to attribute to God and His work any compromise or limitation which might be bettered. Hence, the hesitation which some have about the death and suffering in an evolutionary process, which is effectively the creative work of God.

Furthermore, and for our theme, revelation being conveyed in words which accommodate a flawed human understanding is a problem if this introduces error into the Genesis text. We looked at this latter concern previously. (6.1–3) However, when a final good is achieved as the end of God's purposes, this might be considered a good of pristine perfection. We will return to the scriptural perspective shortly.

From the above preparatory comments, the term 'good' has a varied sense in familiar life. With our artefacts that ranges from functioning effectively to achieve their purpose, which may contribute to further 'goods'. These are functional goods. There may be an ethical and relational sense with an overall contribution to human flourishing, which we might prefer to Aristotle's 'happiness', a final good. These varied goods may be closely connected depending on context, though that of pristine perfection is less common.

Let's take a different example which is not a human artefact. We saw in an earlier chapter how we use functional language about the heart, but we did not introduce the term 'good' at that point. (3.1) Now, we can take that further step.

When the heart is functioning properly, the cardiologist may say concerning various medical tests: "Everything looks good," or more ominously, "this doesn't look so good." Here is a functional sense of 'good' when the heart is doing what it is teleologically there to do.

If not, the consequence may be more than an unhappy patient. If there is serious suffering or disability, an ethical question arises: "Where is God in my suffering?" The physical-biological and functional sense of 'not good' with the heart may take on an ethical and relational dimension of 'not good'.

This starts to suggest that 'good' in some sense is woven into the creation itself. Again, we will return to the question of value woven into the creation.

The above do not exhaust our use of the term 'good'. For example, for most of our artefacts to function effectively, we need good quality workmanship. This is close to, but might be distinguished from a functional good. Also related is that of ability as in saying "she's good at what she does." We can improve on functionality as in "it's good to learn by our mistakes."

Another value closely related to 'good' is that of 'beautiful'. We can say that Juliet's rose and its sweet smell are beautiful and some of the things we make are functionally to achieve something beautiful, such as musical instruments.

The functional good of a musical instrument achieves something of the beautiful if played by a good-ability player in a particular piece of good music. Indeed, a final good may also be a final beauty. As with ethics, this sense of beautiful is certainly connected with feelings and emotions within ourselves.

However, that does not determine that our sense of beauty is confined to our internal emotions or the language of beauty which we learn as part of the linguistic expression of our emotional response.

Accepting this more wide-ranging sense of 'good' and 'beautiful', we will nevertheless stay with the earlier broad categories of the functional, ethical, relational and final sense of 'good'. This is so that we keep sight of our main point, which is to see the creative-constructive aspect as we use the varied term 'good' across different contexts. Pristine perfection however is not a sense of 'good' as we use it in everyday life and the things we make, except perhaps as rhetorical praise—"perfect, well done!"

In summary so far, the term 'good' may be moved across varied contexts of human life and at least some of the world of living systems, showing a varied but also inter-related sense.

'Good' is not merely a metaphor for something else but conveys the reality we experience in our lives. And again, we can use the power of the term 'good' for truth or falsehood and deception, and hence for moral good or evil. We thereby see a complex constructive aspect to our language which is not arbitrary but woven into human life within God's creation.

We turn next to the Genesis creation account and, as before, try to relate this to our varied contemporary use of the term 'good'. There will be a scriptural perspective that much of this 'good' concerns God and our relationship with Him, while there is also considerable similarity between Genesis and our contemporary use.

7.2 God's Creative Work as 'Good' and 'Very Good'

Given this preparatory background to our contemporary and varied use of the term 'good', how does that help us relate to Genesis and the ANE? As we have seen, the term has a wide semantic range in contemporary use. We now consider how the four goods, functional, relational, ethical and final relate to Genesis and God's creative work.

Genesis and a 'Functional Good'

With the ANE scheme of existence which we find in the Genesis creation account, we have seen the close parallel with our own artefacts. (3.2) The scheme of separation, function, name and increased order applies well to both.

We might now expect God's judgement of His work as 'good' to apply in this functional-purpose sense, given the functional ontology of the Genesis account. The work of creation is good in that it is ordered and its varied parts are able to carry out their function as God intended. This is a sense of 'good' we also use in everyday life.

John Walton notes that 'good' has a variety of meanings, not only in our familiar life, but also in scripture. He mentions those we also noted in the previous section on our contemporary use. One example was that of pristine perfection, which some are inclined to attribute to the creation before the fall.

However, on consideration of its use in the Bible, Walton concludes that while this sense of pristine good pertains to God Himself, the word for good in the creation account does not concern pristine perfection.[144] He also considers 'good' in contrast to 'evil', which is an ethical sense with scriptural examples. Again, this does not seem to be the relevant sense in the creation account of Genesis 1.

That returns us to the functional sense of 'good', which Walton considers the relevant sense in the creation account. This functional sense occurs elsewhere in scripture and fits with the functional focus of the creation.[145] Perhaps the clearest indication of the functional sense is shown where Walton considers the case where the man is alone and none of the animals correspond to him. "It is not good for the man to be alone." (Gen.2:18)

---

[144] Walton 2015b, 54.

[145] Examples of 'good' as functional which Walton gives are Ex. 18:17; 2 Chron. 6:27; Ps. 133:1; Prov. 24:23; Is. 41:7. While some of these might be seen as ethical, the Isaiah example is a case of a metalworker completing a piece of work which functions effectively as intended. The fact that Isaiah is mocking the making of an idol does not affect the functional sense of the Hebrew term *ṭôḇ*, 'good' in Genesis.

This 'not good' is clearly not an ethical issue or one of poor workmanship. It is a case where the full functioning of this final element of the ordered creation requires and at first lacks the presence of the woman—not good.[146]

Unless that 'not good' is functionally remedied, humanity cannot fill the world and rule over it, and the man will be lacking a companionship which the animals cannot provide; they are not like him whereas the woman is like him. Hence again, the clearest sense of 'good' in the creation account is that the various components of the creation function as intended as an ordered whole.

This is a now familiar teleological sense that we can again call or name a *functional good.*

But can we go further? While the Genesis focus is on the functional good, there may also be other implicit senses in the text that were not the creation account's central concern, but which should nevertheless have a place.

Genesis and a 'Final Good'

Accepting that 'good' has a functional sense in that the creation functions as God intended, what was His intent? We recall that Aristotle saw varied subsidiary goods contributing towards an overall greater good. That is very often part of our own practices and artefacts. We see something similar in Genesis as the days of creation progress towards the creation of human beings.

What God saw as 'good' finally concludes with what was 'very good'. Hence, a familiar sense of functional 'goods' working towards a greater or 'final good' also seems present in the cumulative functional goods of God's creative work.

But can we go beyond the 'very good' at the end of the creation if that still has only a functional sense? Is there yet more to God's creation than a functional sense of 'good'? To take Walton again:

> "God has established a modicum of order adequate for our survival and for his plan to unfold. There is still a long way to go before the ultimate order of new creation is achieved. People are supposed to be part of that ordering as vice-regents."[147]

---

[146] Walton 2009, 50, 148–149. See also Walton 2015a, 169–170.

[147] Walton 2015b, 56.; 2018, 157.

We see now that what is functionally good is to achieve a further good which does not just stop with the creation of human beings on the sixth day. Our cultural mandate as God's vice-regents is to be part of a further ordering of creation, even perhaps to the ultimate order of a new creation.

That ultimate order will surely embrace human flourishing, well-being and happiness, if we may use that last term. To carry out our mandate in an unfallen world would be a task of deep satisfaction and fulfilment, which will be blessed by God if our mandate is carried out according to His will.

Progress towards further order, and perhaps even an ultimate completed order, whatever that might have been, is surely also a 'good'. It may not be explicit in the text, but it is an obvious corollary to our being vice-regents on God's behalf.

We have then a teleological direction which we should distinguish from the earlier functional good. Let's again call this a 'final good' which includes human happiness, flourishing along with, presumably, further functional and material order culminating in some 'ultimate order of new creation' as Walton puts it above. It may not be explicit in the text, but it is surely latent or implicit in our cultural mandate—a final good.

Genesis and a Relational and Ethical 'Good'

Having mentioned human happiness and flourishing, this is not achieved by socially isolated human beings. We see this when the man finds the woman who corresponds to him; his words are expressions of joy and delight. And similarly, to be with God in the garden in the cool of the evening is surely a time of joyful companionship.

There is a relational aspect between human beings and with God Himself. Those personal relations are present from the start when the implementation of the cultural mandate has barely begun to function. And when it does function and humanity is multiplied, human relations will similarly be multiplied as, hopefully, a further and developing relational good.

To take a different approach to happiness and well-being, with what we call 'the Fall', we have death as a consequence. We return to the dust of the ground, which is a falling away from order to less order and thereby a loss of the functional good. But this would also have brought sadness and grief, even if that is not mentioned in the account.

Since this is a near universal human response, then a subsidiary sense of failure in the ordered good is grief which is opposed to human well-being, flourishing and happiness.

The point is that while 'good' in a functional sense prevails in the Genesis text, a teleological sense towards an overarching or final good is latent, as is a relational good. We might also suppose that an ethical sense of good is not far away, particularly when we consider the blessedness and disruption of the personal-relational between aspect between God and ourselves.

For further clarifications of the term 'good', we turn to the trees in the garden.

7.3 The Trees in the Garden

What was the significance of those two trees in the Garden of Eden, and of eating the fruit of those trees in relation to a sense of 'good'? There was the tree of life and the tree of the knowledge of good and evil. (Gen. 2:9) It seems likely that eating the fruit of the tree of life would lead to immortality—surely a final good to which we will return.

But we start with the latter tree of knowledge, which was understood as the tree of wisdom. I take it that 'wisdom' is equivalent to 'the knowledge of good and evil'.[148]

We might suppose that wisdom will include coming to understand God's ordered creation, since that will enable us to create a further degree of order in line with our cultural mandate. This culminates in modern science and its technological applications, and should also be manifest in our social and personal life. All that has that sense of a *functional good*. Hence, when God declared various components of creation as 'good', it was in that functional sense of doing what was intended in the overall order of creation.

However, there is surely much more to eating this fruit than the functional good of developing our cultural mandate and scientific knowledge arising from wisdom in a practical sense. For example, how do we determine the *ends* to which such knowledge should be applied in both science and social life? Yes, we might achieve *our* intended functional ends, but what *ought* they to be?

---

[148] For the significance of the Garden in the ANE and the relation of the Genesis Trees to God, see Walton 2015b, 116–127. Wenham examines various possible meanings of 'the knowledge of good and evil' and endorses its meaning as wisdom. (Wenham 1987, 63, §5)

We might have knowledge about nuclear physics, but do we apply this to medical practices, energy generation or nuclear weapons? And how do those ends of ours accord with God's purposes, all of which is presumably why we require wisdom?

Hence, a functional good which does what *we in fact intend* may conflict with other goods related to what we *ought to intend*. I trust it is not confusing to say that a functional good might become an ethical 'not-good' or contribute to a final 'not-good' or evil.

This teleological question of ends to be achieved is entirely appropriate since God's creation is itself an intentional functional ontology which is teleologically directed. Our cultural mandate will similarly have a teleological direction, which determines the ends to which we apply our knowledge.

Wisdom requires much more than having informed knowledge and using it in the manufacture of our artefacts and the organisation of society. Wisdom is there so that we adjust our rule as God's stewards to good ends, where 'good' is more than a functional good determined by *our* intentions, goals and ends, which may of themselves turn good into evil.

Hence, a *final good* is implicit in this tree of knowledge or wisdom.

But we need to go further and ask *how we acquire* the wisdom symbolised by that fruit so that our rule achieves human flourishing and the glory of God. Put differently, acquiring wisdom is to ensure that what we intend is aligned with what God intends and moves towards a final good.

We also remember that Adam is an archetype and what he does, we do. This is not about eating fruit but about a principle in human life which has its archetype in Adam's choice. That is, do we make ourselves the authors of judging good and evil, which effectively makes us a source of wisdom? Walton puts it like this:

> "In the ancient Near East, life and wisdom are the prerogatives of the gods that they are reluctant to grant as they try to maintain distance between themselves and humanity. In the Bible, life and wisdom are possessed by God, and they are made available to humans as they are in relation to Him. The trouble comes when humans try to seize them on their own terms."[149]

---

[149] Walton 2015b, 127, 143.

Walton notes the now familiar contrast between the pagan gods and the God of the Hebrews, who is not reluctant to grant life and wisdom in order to maintain a distance between Himself and humanity. Life and wisdom are possessed by God to be made available to us as we are in a relation to Him.

The central issue with eating from that tree of knowledge contrary to God's command, is that we effectively put ourselves in the place of God as the originators of wisdom. And so, the penalty of death which, rather than producing further order in line with God's purposes, we ourselves become disordered and return to the dust.

Hence, the sense of 'good' is also related to achieving wisdom for teleological ends in dependence on God instead of substituting ourselves as the source of wisdom. Rather than proliferating fine distinction in the sense of 'good', let's subsume our reliance on God and in relationship to him for wisdom as a *relational good,* which is also familiar use in human life.

Walton makes that relational point above. However, there may be other factors which are secondary and latent in the text which give a further theological sense of 'good' or further develop the goods noted above, though still with a sense of our relation to God.

The tree was also the tree of *knowledge* of good and evil. This 'knowledge' is not merely about acquiring information regarding God's purposes for creation and ourselves, which is likely how we would understand 'knowledge' at first sight. While the term has a variety of meanings in the Old Testament, some of these are relational.

For example, here Moses says to God in a strongly relational context: "If you are pleased with me, teach me your ways so I may know you and continue to find favour with you." (Ex. 33:13)

We recall again how Walton notes above that life and wisdom are made available to humans in a relation to God, which is the sense of 'I may *know* you' in Moses' remark above.

Being with God in the garden similarly suggests the start of receiving that wisdom from Him within a close relationship.[150] Furthermore, this relational

---

[150] Wenham considers a variety of views, endorsing something similar to the main text. He agrees that the tree of knowledge signifies wisdom and eating the fruit concerns a self-sufficiency of knowledge. However, he does not deal directly with the sense of

aspect also suggests an ethical dimension to the 'good and evil'. To try to obtain the wisdom apart from God is not merely to lose it, which leads to a failure in us functioning as we should. Leaving God aside or taking His place is to violate the relationship, which is to move to the ethical.

To take an analogy, if we betray a close friend who wanted the best for us, we would consider it an ethical failing. As for much of the behaviour related in Genesis which follows eating the fruit, that can certainly be classed as ethical. Hence, it is reasonable to see a latent ethical dimension in the Genesis text, even if it is not the central issue. There is a latent *ethical good* closely associated with a *relational good.*

We might think of this ethical sense in terms of 'sin'. Walton considers this approach, noting the 'sin' also has range of meanings. He avoids theological developments of the term in the church's history and keeps his focus on the Old Testament.

He mentions sin as: crime, a burden to be borne, a debt to be repaid, missing the mark. Walton goes on to consider what sin does, such as alienate or result in disequilibrium.[151]

Given these varied meanings of 'sin' in the Old Testament, an ethical sense is not excluded. Walton notes that many ethical expectations of the ANE were also present in Israel, but the source of these was very different. The heart of Israel's religion was the relationship with God in accord with God's holiness, which was a requirement of the Covenant.[152]

Hence again, this relationship aspect was present or at least latent in eating from the tree of knowledge, since the result was alienation from God, even if it

---

'knowing' as deep personal commitment or relate the tree to the ANE context. (Wenham 1987, 63–64, §5)

A few other examples of a relational sense of 'know'. God says of Abraham: "For I have chosen (known) him, so that he will direct his children and his household after him to keep the way of the LORD by doing what is right and just, so that the LORD will bring about for Abraham what he has promised him." (Gen. 18:19) We read that "Adam knew his wife Eve", meaning sexual intercourse, which is deeply relational. (Gen. 4.1) That sense of knowing is also present in the New Testament, where Jesus will say to some: "Depart from me, I never knew you." (Matt. 7:23) The last of these is hardly about 'knowing' as being informed; Jesus is only too well informed. The problem concerns the absence of a living relationship.

[151] Walton 2015b, 141; 141–148.

[152] Walton 2015b, 146–147.

was not the central meaning of the term 'good'. So also, sin leads in the direction of a broken relationship and hence, we can speak of an *ethical good or evil* in eating the fruit of that tree of the knowledge of good and evil.[153]

The earlier examples of challenges to beliefs which believers and many others hold (6.5), are more explicit consequences coming to us from the archetypal Adam eating the fruit from that tree of knowledge. God and a scriptural context are absent from those challenges and we determine the path of wisdom for ourselves, constructed with the language of virtue and justice.

There is no relation to God or dependence on Him. The result was logical incoherence while increasingly disordering our understanding of the creation and ourselves.

To summarise, given that God declares the major components of creation as 'good' and Genesis understands wisdom by the phrase 'the knowledge of good and evil', it seems right to ask what might be the sense of the term 'good'. The term has varied but inter-related meanings.

There is a *functional good* which achieves what is intended. That implies those intentions should be orientated towards a teleological or *final good*, which involves ourselves through the cultural mandate, being God's vice-regents. As far as the trees are concerned, the central theme of the phrase 'knowledge of good and evil' is wisdom, where we are dependent on God as the source of wisdom within a relation of love and commitment, a *relational good.*

'Knowledge' along with 'good and evil' are also concerned with teleological ends in our cultural mandate, again to achieve a *final good.* An ethical sense to 'good' is not far away, particularly when we see the disruption of the relationship with God due to our eating from the tree of knowledge contrary to God's command, supposing ourselves to be a source of wisdom.

Hence, an *ethical good* is closely associated with a *relational good.* The importance of the relational is conveyed in the use of the term 'knowledge' within the Old Testament. Wisdom is to discern good from evil because to *know* the good is to *love* the good and its originator, God Himself.

We finally note that there are other nuances to 'good', which we will not take any further since they are less significant though present. For example, the

---

[153] The consequence of eating the fruit of the tree of knowledge is usually termed the 'Fall', though Walton notes this is not a scriptural term and does not adequately convey the Genesis sense of the knowledge of good and evil. Walton 2015b, 142 ff.

woman saw that the fruit of the tree of knowledge was good for food and pleasant to the eyes. (Gen. 3:6) This surely includes the everyday satisfaction of taste and nourishment.

That such varied goods are mirrored in familiar human life should not surprise us if the Genesis account relates the most fundamental realities of the creation and the human condition.

7.4 Value Integrated with the Material Creation

There is a philosophical principle which claims that we cannot derive values from facts, or put differently, *what ought to be* from *what is*. Obviously enough, what is good, evil or just are not solutions to a mathematical equation, neither can they be derived from laws of physics.

Values belong to our beliefs about what is experienced in human life. Value-*beliefs* can certainly be investigated. For example, the social sciences investigate what people in fact believe, or what are the consequences of social policies.

However, whatever is implemented as social policy does not tell us what ought to be implemented as policy. While the outcomes of policies can be and are usually investigated, whether these are 'good' in an ethical, relational and value rather than a functional sense is a judgement we make. In this philosophical position, often called the *fact-value* or *is-ought* divide, human values are likely to be reduced from a transcendent or divine origin to what is believed or practiced in human societies and cultures.

And of course, those practices and beliefs will differ between cultures.

This philosophical fact-value divide is particularly prominent in *empiricism*, which holds that knowledge is based on experience which comes to us through our senses, along with logical relations that hold within experience. Empiricism does justice to everyday experience. We can, at least in principle and in some or many cases, determine whether something is true of false in an objective person-independent sense.

We can investigate the facts of the matter and not merely rely on beliefs or opinions. Empiricism also gives a place to scientific knowledge based on testing and evidence. By contrast, since judgements of value are not matters of experience in that factual sense, they are not knowledge and cannot be derived from the facts which we can investigate.

However, as with other examples we have seen, empiricism is self-defeating. It cannot itself be derived from experience and so, it is not knowledge and cannot be known to be true from its own premise.[154]

Certainly, we make judgements about value questions and they are important judgements for us, but the facts of the matter take us no further. It is now a short step to suppose that whatever is creative in our ethical and value-language, that creativity is determined by our interests and concerns, which are also rooted in much wider historical and other factors.

Some would argue that most of the accepted values in a culture come from the interests of dominant social groups which control not only resources but even language itself. We saw examples of this with the challenges. (6.5)

How do we deal with this dichotomy between fact and value, what is and what ought to be? Can we say something more positive than merely criticising empiricism? This returns us to the Genesis creational 'good' and its varied sense, leading to an implicit final good.

If we take a scriptural perspective on language, we must rethink the relation between fact and value in the light of God declaring His creation as 'good', and even as 'very good'. While the primary sense is that of a functional good, a relational, ethical and final sense are latent.

We might even say that a final sense of 'good' is rather more than being latent, since our cultural mandate is to bring further order to achieve some final ordered state.

---

[154] This apparent separation of fact from value is argued by David Hume. We cannot infer an 'ought' from an 'is', in other words, how things ought to be from how they in fact are. (Hume 1985, 521, 3.1.1)

Hume was noted for taking empiricism to its logical conclusion. The operations of the understanding divide into two ('Hume's Fork'): (i) the comparison or relations between ideas such as mathematics, logical relations and linguistic rules such as 'all bachelors are unmarried men'; (ii) inferences of matters of fact which rely on experience, particularly cause and effect. (Ibid. 515, also Hume 1999, 109, 4.1.1–7) In contrast to (i), moral judgements don't arise from the relation between ideas which are the objects of some science. (Hume 1985, 520) As for (ii), values such as what is good or just are not inferred from experience, for example, by investigating the evidence as we do with the facts. Neither is there is an existent real moral entity as moral realism might claim. (Ibid. 519) However, Hume acknowledged we have moral feelings which are important. (Ibid. 521). Nevertheless, these are sentiments of ours and do not alter the fact-value divide.

Given God's assessment of creation as good, value is woven into the material facts of causes, processes and structures. This does not mean such values jump out of the back of an equation or experiment. It is we who make those judgements concerning good and evil. We judge the heart as having a teleological-functional sense of good when it does what it is there to do.

Similarly, it is we who make judgements about what is beautiful or ugly. It is Juliet who judges the rose and its sweet smell as something having a beauty-value and turns this into a metaphor for her love of Romeo. She does this in a social context where most of us feel similarly about the rose and hence her metaphorical use is persuasive while also being inadequate.

Even hard-boiled mathematicians or scientists may comment on the simplicity or elegance of their proofs and theories. Sometimes, such elegance is even considered a possible indicator of truth. These are variations of aesthetic value judgements of goodness and beauty going beyond our feelings to being integral to the creation.

Perhaps most importantly, we accord dignity and value to human beings, though unfortunately, that has never been so universally. Slave-owning cultures are ever present and Dalits (untouchables) are still with us today. Yet even here, value judgements are made by ourselves, which is then how we see the world.

However, our value judgements are not confined to beliefs within social and cultural structures. They reflect the reality of creation but are discerned and articulated by ourselves in a language which differs from material-fact language. For example, the use of terms 'ought' and 'is' as well as the language of 'good' and 'beautiful' differs from that of material objects, causes and effects.

What is it that enables this discernment where we bring together such different ways of speaking? It is again the image of God within ourselves which discerns God's integration of fact and value within His creation. It is also that image which enables us to speak of and implement good, evil, beauty and justice in our own practices.

That discernment is essential if we are to take the creation order to a further or final good as part of our cultural mandate. We will then mirror God's integration of fact and value in our own endeavours and the cultural mandate. To do all this, we must be dependent on the source of wisdom, namely God Himself.

Tragically, a consequence of our participation in the archetypal Adam is that we seek, as he did, to make ourselves the originators of wisdom. Through Adam, we have also eaten the fruit from the tree of knowledge. And so, we lost access not only to wisdom but also to the tree of life—that truly final good.

But if we failed to achieve a final good through our cultural mandate and lost access to the tree of life, God's purposes for a final good remain. Indeed, such a final good will likely incorporate all other variants of 'good', perhaps even that of pristine perfection.

And that final good will be achieved by a full and perfect obedience to the will and wisdom of God, though it will not be through our obedience but that of another. Indeed, wisdom from God is even now available to us, along with access to the tree of life.

We can then look to this final good with confidence, which Aristotle only dimly apprehended and Adam along with ourselves failed to achieve. However, it will be achieved through Jesus Christ:

> "On each side of the river stood the tree of life, bearing twelve crops of fruit, yielding its fruit every month. And the leaves of the tree are for the healing of the nations. No longer will there be any curse." (Rev. 22:2–3)[155]

7.5 'Good' and Our Linguistic Creativity

We conclude by returning to our linguistic theme. The term 'good' has a range of meanings which are not unique to us, for example, they are present in the ethical philosophy of Aristotle. Whatever we think of Aristotle's wider philosophy, we share much of the sense of 'good' which he identified.

Furthermore, some of those meanings are reflected in the Genesis creation account. Or perhaps better, our use of the term reflects God's work in creation.

As God progresses the creation, He declares the early states as 'good', and finally 'very good'. This use of 'good' is most likely a functional sense with creation functioning as God intended, which is a similar use to our artefacts. But there is also a teleological progress in the creation, suggesting a teleological or final good.

When it comes to the tree of 'the knowledge of good and evil', this phrase is closely connected with obtaining wisdom, which is to discern the purposes of God for us. We might equally say those purposes concern the teleological ends

---

[155] Ian Paul makes various connections between Genesis, Revelation and other Old Testament passages in his Commentary. (Paul 2018, 358–359)

we are to achieve, which is again suggesting progress towards a final good for creation and ourselves.

However, the central issue with that tree of knowledge is that we should receive our wisdom from God within a relationship to Him, rather than originating it from ourselves—a relational good. Then, since receiving wisdom depends on our relationship God, disrupting that relationship introduces an ethical sense of good.

Such varied senses to the term 'good' show a creative-constructive linguistic ability to connect various contexts of our lives by moving the term 'good' between contexts. These include different contexts of everyday life, which are also mirrored in Genesis as it speaks about God, creation and ourselves.

Furthermore, in living and experiencing those contexts, their reality is conveyed or evoked in ourselves. That lived experience is perhaps most pronounced with the pain and terror of rampant evil, apparently heading towards a final not-good, whether that comes from other persons or from nature itself. That the world should fall into disorder or even non-order was also a significant concern in the ANE, as it will be for us, particularly in times of war and social instability.

Our linguistic creativity is also shown in the difference in sense between the language of value, ethics and morals and the language of facts and experience. We noted the philosophical fact-value divide, which certainly recognises that difference in sense.

However, it is our linguistic creativity that enables us to connect fact with value in the way we speak and act. In doing so, we again mirror the creative speaking of God, who declared His creation as 'good' and 'very good'. It is God who integrates fact and value, which we recognise by articulating it in language and implementing it in our individual lives, wider social practices and artefacts.

Genesis is also an archetypal metanarrative showing itself through all human societies, cultures and history. It is then unsurprising that other cultures have similar understandings, as we saw with Aristotle in relation to our own use of the term 'good' and our ability to relate to its varied sense in Genesis.

One might object that some of those meanings are marginal to the text and a potential diversion from what is central. Even if there is a constructive aspect to our understanding, are we in danger of over-constructing the text so to speak? This is a fair objection and should act as a caution.

It is similar to the warning of reading our own cultural background into the Genesis text, or into the literature from other ages or cultures. Nevertheless, we share a common humanity and live in the same created world where the Genesis creation account unfolds in human history and our cultural mandate.

Hence, what is secondary or latent in the text should not escape our attention since even the latent will affect us. It is in that origin account that the whole human condition is present in embryonic form.

There is one last point to close this chapter. We should recall that God accommodates the human faculties which He placed within us as the image of God and that cultural mandate to be His vice-regents. Hence, God accommodates revelation to human understanding within human cultures and language, which may include erroneous understanding within our mandate to rule. We saw this with the three-tiered universe. (6.1–3)

However, accommodation does not include error in our relation to God, which is not our mandate to rule. Nor does accommodation include our constructions of human significance, values and the image of God. That does not stop us constructing God or gods in our own image, but such is a result of the archetypal Adam eating the fruit from the tree of knowledge.

With the creative ability of language, we too readily turn good into evil, truth into falsehood and justice into oppression as we rely on our own wisdom. We are sufficiently creative to maintain the language of virtue while changing the underlying practices. The creative power of our language may even make those new practices virtuous; we have created a new reality—for good or evil.

We finally turn to consider not merely that we speak about God, but *how* we speak about and to Him within a proper context. Our creative-constructive use of language must now be re-directed from the creation to the Creator who is beyond our investigation and understanding.

8. The Scriptural Context: Speaking About and to God

We now come to consider language when speaking about God, and indeed, to God. We have done a fair amount of speaking about God already, but without giving much thought to *how* this is possible. After all, we are speaking about a being who is not part of this created order.

We recall that was one of the great contrasts between the God of the Hebrews and the gods of the ancient Near East (ANE), who were part of the creation or were born into it. How do we speak about and to God through familiar language rooted in this world, without confusing God with the world, given the creative power of our language?

A reasonable answer is that our speaking about God is metaphorical. Here are just a few examples: God as my rock (Ps. 18:2); The Lord is my shepherd (Ps. 23:1); God as a potter (Is. 64:8); sun and shield (Ps. 84:11); evergreen cypress (Hos. 14:8); arm and ear (Is. 59:1); hand and arm (Ps. 89:10, 98:1).

Given that our theme is language, another example of metaphor comes from the creation account: "And God *said,* 'Let there be …'" God's *speaking* is surely a metaphor. We will hardly suppose that God uttered these words in Hebrew or perhaps some angelic language.

Neither does it make sense to ask *how* God learnt the language or *when* He spoke the words, which does make sense in our case as we saw with St Augustine. The point is to recognise God's creative power by means of this anthropomorphic metaphor of 'speaking'. It is that metaphor which allows us to believe in God as the Creator where God's creative 'speaking' is in its divine character incomprehensible to us.

Hence, while we have a metaphor of God's creative speaking, we cannot relate the metaphor directly to the transcendent-divine reality. Contrast this with Juliet making her point from the rose's sweet smell in relation to the person

Romeo. The rose itself, the resulting rose metaphor and the reality of Romeo and her love for him were all well understood by Juliet and by us, so that the metaphor could make Juliet's point.

We might instead say that God's creative speaking is analogical language. It functions as analogies do, with both similarities and differences in sense. And again, that seems true.

However, we still need to ask *how* any metaphors and analogies about God are constrained to convey the truth, given that we have no immediate access to God's transcendent reality to check this. One answer which has run throughout this book, is that such speaking must be set within the scriptural context.

While we have a mandate to investigate the created order and rule within our domain, we do not have any such mandate with the being of God. Rather, we turn to the Bible, which is a proper context to give sense to any metaphors, analogies or other theological language.

But *how* does this contextual control work? We need something more than talk about metaphors, analogies and even the scriptural context. *How* is the sense contextually constrained when applied to God which differs from the sense of the original and familiar use in human life?

I will approach these questions through the topic of *logic*, where God is logically different from His creation. This logic shows itself in how we speak of Him in contrast to how we speak about familiar life.

In this final chapter, we will see how that logic works within human language and our speaking about God. The logic we use in familiar everyday speaking, if applied to God, will likely lead to nonsense and we need to know why that is. We start with such a case.

8.1 Speaking About God (i): An Example of Philosophical Nonsense

A course in the philosophy of religion is likely to deal with God's omnipotence, which may be introduced with this specific example. "God can supposedly do anything He wills, but He cannot do *absolutely* anything. For example, He cannot make a square circle. Even God cannot bring about a logical contradiction."

There then follows a further example designed to examine whether God's omnipotence is logically coherent. This following example is hardly a sophisticated theological (or philosophical) statement of omnipotence, but it well illustrates the problems arising from a loss of context.

George Mavrodes considers whether God can create a stone which is too heavy for Him to lift. Suppose God can create such a stone, then it seems He is not omnipotent since He cannot lift this stone. On the other hand, if God cannot create such a stone, then again it seems there is something He cannot do, which is to create a stone which He cannot lift.

The thrust of this argument is that the concept of God's omnipotence is incoherent since in both cases, we start with God being omnipotent but end up with something even He cannot do.

Having outlined the problem of the heavy stone, Mavrodes argues that there are no implications on God's omnipotence since the stone has within itself an implicit contradiction. Suppose God is omnipotent and can indeed create a stone which is too heavy for Him to lift.

Then it seems we have a stone which even God cannot lift when His omnipotence presumably determines He can lift anything. The stone described by this contradiction is impossible and therefore has nothing to do with the doctrine of divine omnipotence. Indeed, Mavrodes notes that it is God's omnipotence which makes such a stone a contradictory impossibility.[156]

By contrast, Harry Frankfurt considers whether God can indeed bring about a contradiction. While we might not be able to conceive this, some philosophers have rejected the principle that God cannot bring about what is contradictory. So, suppose that God creates a stone which is too heavy for Him to lift.

Being omnipotent, He might then proceed to lift it! If this stone is problematic in the first place because it is already self-contradictory as Mavrodes argues above, then a second contradiction in God lifting such a stone is hardly any more objectionable and may even be possible with God.[157]

We need not be detained by arguments about square circles and the like. If an object is square, it cannot in the same aspect be circular. Furthermore, we have no idea what a 'square circle' *is* or can possibly *be*; how do we even recognise such a bizarre unknowable?

Similarly in the case of the heavy stone, the above arguments not only posit a conceptual absurdity, they go on to hypothetically objectify this heavy stone into an existent pseudo-entity, which questions God's ability to make it. Even if

---

[156] Mavrodes 2007, 146–148.

[157] Frankfurt 1964, 262–263.

this is only a thought experiment, it is not so much the contradiction as the loss of a proper context and the accompanying sense which renders the heavy stone as non-sense irrelevant to God's omnipotence.

The theistic resonance of terms like 'God' and 'omnipotence' does not of itself locate the discussion in a proper context which does justice to the being of God and the difference between the Creator and creation.

In this example, the context is not merely inadequate, it is wholly misplaced since the arguments are contextually located within our own abilities to make things which we may or may not be able to lift. This is then projected onto God. How does that make sense; is it clear what it means for God, who is Eternal Spirit and the Creator of all things, to 'lift a heavy stone'?

Even if the stone only illustrates a logical point, the illustration is misleading because the question is contextually framed and subsequent arguments shaped by our familiar life. God's omnipotence resists philosophical examination by us imposing everyday concepts with which we make sense of our lives in this world.

When language is taken out of a context of understood application, sense is lost and philosophical problems thrive, as do philosophical arguments.[158]

While this contradiction of the heavy stone is amusing, there is a serious side to it. Many believers, including philosophers and theologians, have attenuated God's omnipotence in order to maintain the integrity of processes in creation and particularly our human will, choice and actions.

For example, one might argue that God has given us free-will, whereas for God, it is a hands-off affair so to speak, though there may still be a lame concession that God can bring good out of evil to mitigate the consequences of our foolish or sinful choices.

So, how do we deal with this more serious logical question in a proper scriptural context so that our speaking is constrained while still making sense?

---

[158] A classic example of this philosophical nonsense is in Plato's *Euthyphro* where Socrates seeks clarification: "The point which I should first wish to understand is whether the pious or holy is beloved by the gods because it is holy, or holy because it is beloved of the gods" (Plato 2013). This conundrum requires a proper context which does not come from human life or from the gods, who are bigger versions of ourselves. Neither Socrates nor Plato had a proper scriptural context for the being of God.

8.2 Speaking About God (ii): Making Sense from the Scriptural Context

Let's reconsider God's omnipotence or better, consider the *sovereignty* of God, to use a term more familiar to believers. 'Omnipotence' is a rather abstract philosophical term whereas 'sovereignty' is related to a Sovereign who, hopefully in the case of an earthly ruler, rules for the good of others.

Here we confine ourselves to a question often at the heart of debates on God's sovereignty: if God works in human affairs to achieve His will, is our will and responsibility then compromised by God's will?

We recall the story in the Bible, how Joseph, a favourite son, was hated by his brothers. They initially wanted to kill him but then decided to sell him as a slave. (Gen. 37) After many twists and turns, Joseph ends up as a high official in Pharaoh's court. Finally, Joseph is reconciled to his brothers and says to them: "You intended to harm me, but God intended it for good." (Gen. 50:20)

What might we say about Joseph's brothers? The evil they did was *their* responsibility; it was *their* hatred, *their* choice, *their* intention to harm Joseph by *their* actions. Joseph doubtless stirred up their hatred by his arrogance as a favourite son, which was *his* responsibility, but that does not detract from what the brothers did.

So, let's put a firm marker in the ground; the brothers' choice and actions were truly their own. Furthermore, let's take it that the same went for everyone else in the story, including Joseph himself. If we want to speak of free-will, then everyone exercised their free-will. God did not compromise human responsibility by interfering with anyone's will, choice or subsequent actions.

The problem is where this leaves the will of God. How could God possibly achieve what He intended without violating, interfering with, or overriding human intentions in some way? Perhaps God brought about the circumstances where the actions of the individuals in the story were freely chosen by them to align the outcome with His will.

This might maintain human integrity.[159]

However, it merely shifts the question back to the integrity of surrounding circumstance, including presumably the intentions of others. Hence, if we ask

---

[159] The brief comment in the main text alludes to the thought of the Jesuit Luis Molina (1535–1600). It is part of the larger philosophical question of Future Contingents. An online discussion is in Øhrstrøm and Hasle (2020).

the question: '*How* did God accomplish His will?' we seem to hit insuperable problems given the fixed marker about God not over-riding or in some way interfering with human intentions.

Here is something which I suggest makes sense, though I put it somewhat negatively following our example of Joseph and his brothers; *when human beings intend evil and carry it out, they are wholly responsible for their choices and actions, which are truly their own. Equally, they unfailingly advance the purposes of God.*

That's it. There is no explanation to the question *how* God gets people to advance His purposes, even when they go against what they know He requires. From the perspective of our language and beliefs, we have a rule for the way we use the term 'God', which is not an explanation *how* God's will is accomplished.

Put differently, that rule is part of what we mean by 'God'. The rule maintains human choice and responsibility *and* that God's purposes are fulfilled through those choices, without God being the author of anyone's folly or sin. The rule also rejects any theological determinist or 'whatever will be, will be' fatalist understanding of mankind's predicament.

Where does this rule come from? The words and life of Joseph in the Bible *show the rule*. We cannot explain this rule any further since that is to explain something of the ineffable (beyond understanding) being of God. However, by faith we can accept that the rule makes sense of God, and reflect on the Bible's many examples of God's working, and how such examples might apply to us.

I have not used Joseph's words as an isolated proof text; my use of his words is consistent with the context of this extensive story showing the accomplishment of God's purposes in the affairs of mankind.[160]

Let's put this differently; the *rules* for what makes sense are what we call *logic*. We are thinking about the logic of God, what it makes sense, conceptually, for us to say about Him. Someone might object that I am being illogical, because it is not logically possible for God's will to prevail without some interference with, or compromise of our will. So, the question then becomes: who decides what it makes sense to say about God?

The answer which much of the historic Christian faith commends is that human reason is not the final judge of this question; the Bible determines what it makes sense to say about God.

---

[160] Additional examples are: Acts 2:23; also 3:17,18; 4:27,28. These involve the death of Christ, which is much more significant than the case of Joseph and his brothers.

Put differently, the logic of God requires and arises from a proper context, where believers' beliefs and the more formal doctrinal statements of the church are based on and woven together with the witness of the Bible, which governs belief and reason with respect to God's being, His purposes and work.

We can think about it like this; when Satan and his agents go about like roaring lions, the purposes of God are not frustrated but advanced. This is most striking with the Crucifixion, where the evil deeds of human beings and the influence of Satan are painfully apparent.

Yet, all this evil, to believers the greatest evil ever committed, accomplished the will of God. Human sin is atoned through the life and sacrificial death of Christ which satisfies the justice of God, reconciliation with God is achieved in those who believe, the power and reign of death is overcome, all is ready for Christ's resurrection and triumph and much more besides. It is true, but far too weak to say that God brought good out of evil, rather:

> "This man was handed over to you by God's deliberate plan and foreknowledge; and you, with the help of wicked men, put him to death by nailing him to the cross." (Acts 2:23)

God's sovereignty is affirmed, along with human responsibility.

At this point, a philosopher may ask for a definition of 'free-will', 'human responsibility', 'divine sovereignty' and so forth. Definitions might then lead to a better analysis of the scope, limits and interaction between human freedom and God's omnipotence.

I have no objections to further definitions, for example, we should distinguish between God's omnipotent will dealt with so far, often termed His 'secret' will, and His revealed will known to us by His commandments and in our conscience. The latter is frequently violated, as in the account of Joseph's life.

However, my purpose is to outline the logic within which *any* definitions and subsequent discussions should reside. Put differently, both arguments and definitions need to attend to the context of scripture along with its logic, since changing the logic is to change what it means to be God, potentially changing the character of the Christian faith.

To conclude by returning to language, since no one knows what a square circle or the heavy stone *is* ontologically, arguments relating these to God are entirely constructed from familiar words put together in a superficially plausible and creative way.

However, it does not give us a convincing understanding of the sovereignty of God or how God is logically different from His creation. Even where our language is creative, that is not of itself enough to get us to the truth because such language is governed by a logic embedded in our familiar lives.

By contrast, the logic of God needs to be determined from a scriptural context and will likely look significantly different from that of our familiar life.

Hence, I rejected the contradictions of the square circle and the heavy stone, which had no adequate context to make sense of the sovereignty of God. While the logic of God is different, it is not contradictory because what counts as a contradiction needs a proper context, or if there is no proper context, we are likely talking nonsense.

8.3 The Logic of God: Logic and Sense Woven into Life and Worship

Logic may at first sight seem an abstruse subject. Perhaps we have seen a textbook on logic with all those peculiar symbols which most of us hardly ever come across and certainly don't use in everyday life, except perhaps with some basic arithmetic.

We won't deal with such symbolic logic and will confine ourselves to more familiar matters. We have already made one brief reference to logic when looking at simple arithmetic addition. (5.4)

The point then was to illustrate the way language and logic are embedded in our lives and our judgements. There was a constructing aspect even to simple addition. (5.4) This is a theme which continues, but now within a scriptural context. I take and develop the following example from Gareth Moore.[161]

Suppose a prayer meeting takes place in a room with say six believers. We remember Jesus' promise:

[161] This example comes originally from Gareth Moore. (Moore 1996, 58–67, 80–102) The underlying approach of holding in front of us the actual practices on our lives and how these make sense is an emphasis in Wittgenstein's philosophical approach.

"Again, truly I tell you, if two of you on earth agree about anything they ask for, it will be done for them by my Father in heaven. For where two or three come together in my name, there am I with them." (Matt. 18:20)[162]

For convenience, I will abbreviate this to Jesus being 'present' with them. Since Christians believe in the Trinity, we can also say that God is present by His Spirit. Now, suppose there is an empty chair in the room. These believers are praying to God, but no one addresses the chair as if God the Father or Jesus himself was sitting on it; what an absurd thought!

Suppose someone said: "God is watching over us." Would anyone then look up at the ceiling as if God was 'up there' looking down? It just makes no sense to do so. I am not theorising anything, but *describing* the linguistic and behavioural practices of this prayer meeting which shows that God's presence is not like the presence of anything or anyone else in the room.

Let's now ask how many persons are present at the prayer meeting. We would say there are six; we could name them, say when they arrived, where they sat, what they said, when they left and so on. That is part of the context which gives a sense to someone 'being present' in the room.

But we would not say there were seven persons in the room, namely our six believers *plus* God. Or perhaps there are nine persons since God is a Trinity of persons. God's presence is not established like that of the six who are present.

So, to add God to the six persons in the room makes no sense because such an arithmetical addition only makes sense within a context of language and practices where we establish who is spatially and temporally located inside the room. Since God is not amenable to those practices, it makes no sense to add Him to the number of those who are in the room.

As before, God is logically different from anything else in the room.

Can we perhaps say God is present but His is an *invisible* presence? Suppose you are in a room at night. The atmosphere is creepy, the temperature drops, the floorboards start creaking and the door which was locked suddenly springs open. From the perspective of everyday sense-experience, there is nothing to detect

[162]The immediately preceding context concerns church discipline, where the assurance of Matt. 18:20 includes such a situation. Nevertheless, given that Matt. 18:19 embraces 'anything you ask for', verse 18:20 reasonably takes a wider scope to a prayer meeting and worship more generally, even if only a few are present.

apart from the creepy things going on in the room, but we might well say a ghost entered the room; an invisible presence *came into the room!*

I will leave aside the question whether there is 'really' a ghost in the room. Instead, let's compare this supposed ghostly presence with God's presence.

Most obviously, God's presence at the prayer meeting is not accompanied by any strange phenomena in the room. There have been physical manifestations of God's presence, such as the burning bush or the tongues of fire at Pentecost, but that is usually not the case, even though God is present with believers at prayer.

As for the ghost, suppose we say the ghost is in this room but not in the room next door. This makes sense since it may be that someone next door didn't notice anything untoward in their room. There are ways of speaking which make sense of the ghost being in this room but not next door.

But what applies to an invisible ghost does not apply to God; it makes no sense to say that God is (or is not) *in* the room next door, as if He also came in through the door!

I am not asking anyone to believe in ghosts, but to look at the contrast between the ways we use language within different contexts. There are contexts where it just makes no sense to say something whereas in other contexts it does. We can say things about people in rooms and even about ghosts when none of that makes sense of God.

On the other hand, the context of the prayer meeting in connection with the Bible and Jesus' own words do make sense of God being present with our believers at prayer; they are speaking (and hopefully also listening) to Him and He hears them.

Hence, God's presence is established in a very different way, and therefore gives a different sense of 'being present'. Those contrasts show how God is *logically* different from anything else which exists. The logic shows itself by excluding ways of speaking about God as making no sense, whereas other ways of speaking about Him do make sense but make no sense when speaking about anything other than God.

And so, we again encounter the rule or logic that the Creator is different from the creation. That difference shown in familiar Christian practices, worship and the language employed, the doing and saying woven together, now also woven together with scripture.

Language has that creative power to express logical truths, and these can be applied to God provided the proper context is maintained. The result is a somewhat different logic from everyday applications, in this case of someone being 'present'.

We also note that any metaphorical or analogical sense is now closer to the reality than anyone else being 'present' in the room. God's presence is closer personal one than any human relation, including Juliet's metaphorical rose applied to Romeo.

Hence, we also see that if 'present' has a metaphorical sense when applied to God, it shows the enormous variety that is possible in the sense of the metaphors we use. However, here the work is done by the logic of the scriptural context which controls the sense of any metaphors, while also linguistically expressed, woven together and understood within the practices of familiar life and worship.

8.4 Speaking to God: What's in a Name?

Before considering how we address God when speaking to Him, let's first say something about how we address each other—by name.

The significance of someone's name is not as great for us as for that ancient world, including the significance of names in the Old Testament. Juliet was right at least as far as that goes in our contemporary culture. Nevertheless, names still have significance, and not just for Juliet.

For example, we might use a nickname which often indicates a close and affectionate friendship and understanding of a person. Equally, a nickname may be derogatory. Names used within the family also express a close bond; we might think of 'mum' and 'dad'.

While names are used to identify an individual, a person's name might also be used to damage them, as someone may say: "My name is mud in those circles." That was so in the case of Romeo and Juliet's family names.

Taking another example, in some languages, to address someone who is not well-known or close family by the singular of 'you' is not acceptable. That is the case with Dutch. This is not merely a matter of learning a social convention as one might do in school.

For a native speaker of such a language, there is a definite sense of social discomfort in using an inappropriate form of address. Then in more formal situations we might use a surname. There are also formal titles such as 'Your

Majesty', 'Sir', 'Lady', 'Your Honour' and so forth. These may well be accompanied by some further level of behavioural deference.

When we considered the ANE's conception of existence, we noted the importance of the name, which represents and conveys the function of the named object. We don't give that significance to the names we use of natural objects, though there is a similarity with the biological sciences and of course, the use of functions and names in our own artefacts.

Now however, with the above brief examples of the varied use of personal names, we again see that names can be closely related to an aspect of the person in the way they function in their roles or significance for us. That is so even if the name is thought to be less significant for us than it was in the ANE.

It is not merely a question of learning social conventions. These conventions are learnt from childhood where the doing and saying are woven together, as with St Augustine earlier. Hence those names convey the realities of human life and relationships.

That brings us to addressing God or one of the persons of the Trinity. Some of the names we use have a significance in our familiar life. When using such familiar names to address God, there is also a metaphorical and often logical aspect to the name.

For example, familiar family names convey the family relation and fatherly care and protection we have with God. An example is the opening of the Lord's prayer which leads us to address God as 'Our Father in Heaven' or just 'Heavenly Father'.

This may become more affectionate as with the Aramaic family use of 'Abba', which is closer to 'daddy' than Father. Many believers might be uncomfortable with such a familiar use themselves, as is the case with using the inappropriate and overly familiar singular 'you' in some languages.

That again shows the significance conveyed in the name. If Augustine used a familiar family name for parents and close relations, those are social practices learnt from early life. However, on the three occasions we encounter 'Abba' in the New Testament, it is followed by 'Father', reminding us that we are speaking to God as our Father.[163]

---

[163] Mark 14:36; Rom. 8:15; Gal. 4:6.

Turning to logic, rather than using a theorising approach we take an example woven into human life. Imagine a child saying to its mother: "Does daddy always think of me?"

The reply might be: "Daddy often thinks about you, but not when he's busy at work."

The child's reply might now be: "Does God think about me when He's busy at work?" The question makes no sense of God whereas it does for the child's father. The child has not yet grasped the logical difference between God and ourselves. This logic also shows the metaphorical aspect of the name 'Father', where metaphors may relate remote phenomena as well as close ones.

Perhaps it is right to say that God as our Father is a different but closer relation that that of human fathers and certainly that of the remote metaphor of Juliet's rose and its sweet smell is to the person Romeo and those family names. Our language is able to express the close as well as the more distant metaphor.

Let's next consider the frequently used title 'Lord'. This term is perhaps most often on the lips of believers when addressing God in prayer and worship, and when addressing Christ. In the New Testament, the term is largely uncomplicated and translates the Greek 'kurios', which was used for someone having authority.

However, in the background lies the Old Testament where the names of God were numerous. Many are variants on the unspoken 'YHWH' and the word for God 'El'. Such variants show something of the action or character of God, which is what we might expect from a name, particularly in the context of the ANE.[164]

The name 'YHWH' occurs numerous times throughout the Old Testament. It was the name given to Moses at the burning bush. (Ex. 3:13–16) While the name was present before this time, it was not known in the way it would shortly be revealed in God's deliverance of Israel from slavery in Egypt.[165] Hence again, the name itself conveyed an aspect of God's being and character.

---

[164] For example: YAHWEH-SHALOM: The Lord our Peace: Judges 6:24. EL SHADDAI: God Almighty, Gen. 17:1; 28:3; Ex. 6:2–3.

[165] Some examples before the time of Moses and the burning bush are Gen. 2:4; 4:1; 4:26; 12:8; 13:4; 15:7. 17:1.

Some argue that there is a contradiction with that earlier use and a statement like "I am the LORD. I appeared to Abraham, to Isaac and to Jacob as God Almighty, but by my name the LORD (YHWH) I did not make myself fully known to them." (Ex. 6:3, 4) This book is not the place for an extensive discussion. I merely note that while the name was

Finally, the name of Jesus conveys what is central to his work: "She will give birth to a son, and you are to give him the name Jesus, because he will save his people from their sins." (Matt. 1:21) The name 'Jesus' is etymologically related to Joshua with a Semitic root meaning to deliver or rescue.

This name was also related to 'Emmanuel', God with us, from Isaiah. (Isa. 7:14) These names convey who Jesus was, and to make a logical point, who Jesus *is*.[166]

We might say that in all these cases, the name is not merely a reference to a divine being. In that ANE scheme of separation, function and name, the names of God and of Jesus convey to us an aspect of their being who they are, something of the reality of God including the way God acts, and that further includes God's acts through Jesus Christ. The name 'Jesus' is inseparable from everything he *is*.

To summarise in terms of two of our linguistic themes.

Firstly, I have used the term 'construct' for the creative aspect of human language in relation to the image of God and our cultural mandate. However, when it comes to speaking about and to God and with the names of God, any constructing on our part must lie within the context of scripture.

There is a metaphorical use where words and names are moved from human life to the being of God; that creative linguistic ability continues. But now there is a different *logical* aspect to this. We are no longer dealing with the domain over which Adam and those following him are to rule.

We have here the logic of God, with examples in the previous sections. Even then however, that logic is embedded within our language, showing us what it makes sense to say and what does not make sense. If this logic is constructed within language, it is also contextually constrained by scripture.

Secondly, another theme is that language makes sense through the doing and saying woven together in the practices of human life. Unsurprisingly then, the names of God remain very much anchored in those human practices. That includes the example of family life and worship, but also going beyond that to the experience of God in the history of Israel and the church.

---

known from earlier times in contexts which showed God's power, for example with the birth of Isaac (Gen. 17:1), God unbounded power in deliverance would now be revealed in the Exodus. (See Keil and Delitzsch, 1975, 466–468. See also Walton 2018, 52–53)

[166] Also: "And he will be called Wonderful Counsellor, Mighty God, Everlasting Father, Prince of Peace." (Isaiah 9:6)

Even so, it is as we look at our familiar use of language that we again see the logical difference between creation and the Creator, here our human and heavenly Father.

To close with a final comment on naming. Regardless of our contemporary view of the significance of a person's name, including Juliet's view, there is an enduring and transcendent scriptural perspective on the names of God and of Jesus Christ.

Juliet asked: "What's in a name?"

"Therefore, God exalted him to the highest place
and gave him the name that is above every name,
that at the name of Jesus every knee should bow,
in heaven and on earth and under the earth,
and every tongue acknowledge that Jesus Christ is Lord,
to the glory of God, the Father."

(Phil. 2:9–11)

9. Conclusion: With a Wider Cultural Perspective

A good name is more desirable than great riches;
to be esteemed is better than silver or gold.
(Prov. 22:1)

"What's in a name?"

While Juliet was inclined to see a name as a mere ephemeral label to reference something or someone more substantial, the Psalmist takes a different view. A name, within a context of human life, can convey the character of a person, where the name itself is enough to determine how a person is perceived by others. The significance of a name in the Genesis context within the ancient Near East (ANE) would likely be part of the Psalmist's understanding.

And since Adam and we ourselves name human artefacts, natural objects, persons, behaviours and values, this can be for good or evil, truth or falsehood, clarity or obfuscation, deliberate or unintentional.

Our naming mirrors God's own naming of the structures of creation, where in the ANE the name even completes a thing's existence. Hence, a name has a creative power which may be partly constructed by us. This creative ability belongs to the image of God in ourselves and our cultural mandate. But the name also refers to and is embedded in an ordered creation which we cannot evade.

That, in a nutshell, summarises this book.

However, my conclusion should do a little more to draw the varied material of the book together, so I will focus on two areas.

First, there is a potential dilemma which lies at the heart of this book. On the one hand, I have developed the creative-constructive aspect of language. On the other hand, I have stressed that any constructing by us must take place within a proper context. However, these two aspects might be at odds as we emphasise one side at the expense of the other.

For example, our creative constructions might eliminate God's work in creation as mere constructions of ours and nothing more. Even the existence of God might be similarly eliminated. This is rightly a serious matter for believers, particularly given current cultural trends in many Western societies. A post-truth ideology would confine our constructions within a cultural context.

As a reaction against this, believers might be tempted to minimise the creative aspect of language by seeing in the scriptural context a fixed created order, thereby losing sight of the full scope in our role as God's vice-regents. The image of God in ourselves might now be diminished.

Secondly, since I have tried to show the relevance of my theme, it seems appropriate to conclude with a final focus on relevance. Our contemporary culture has some remarkable examples from wider trends in which many Western churches and believers find themselves. We are not confined to a subject from a remote and ancient past, interesting to scholars perhaps, but largely irrelevant to the society in which we live.

It is beyond the scope of this book to discuss contemporary trends in detail. My purpose in this conclusion is to show the present-day relevance of my linguistic theme arising from its roots in Genesis.

9.1 Resolving a Dilemma

To start with the potential dilemma. On the one hand, I have given prominence to the creative power of our language by using the term 'construct'. There is an extremely varied linguistic-constructive activity on our part through which we see the world, including what the sciences have shown us.

Furthermore, we also make judgments about value, significance, good and evil. We ourselves form those judgements, though they do not take place in a vacuum. Our judgements are formed within a context of surrounding social beliefs and practices, as well as more personal factors.

We saw this social context with St Augustine learning the names of things in childhood. (2.1) Nevertheless, they are our judgements which shape the way we understand ourselves and the world we inhabit. Hence the term 'construct'.

On the other hand, I have also tried to show that this constructing on our part is anchored in human life within the world where we find ourselves. From a Christian worldview, that means we are placed within God's creation, which is an ordered creation with purpose and value woven into the material processes and structures of creation.

Hence, the constructing aspect of our understanding lies within the constraints and possibilities of what God has ordered for our good. Particularly when considering God Himself along with human value and significance, any constructing on our part also needs to be led by scripture.

While this is now familiar territory, the dilemma shows itself in that we are easily driven to over-emphasise either our constructing or God's ordering in a way which distorts our humanity. In both cases, we can distort the image of God and our mandate to rule as His vice-regents. I will illustrate this with a few examples from contemporary cultural trends.

A construct approach may develop a life of its own, potentially leaving ourselves as the final arbiters of significance and truth. One direction this takes is that the individual personal self becomes that final arbiter. For example, an individual self may determine who and what their 'self' *is*, ontologically, since that self does the constructing.

This is striking with questions around gender and sexuality, and is a powerful trend in Western cultures from which such 'selves' are not isolated.[167] As with all trends and social practices, we should ask how these relate to eating the fruit of that tree of the knowledge of good and evil.

Given that this tree is best understood as the tree of wisdom, have we now made ourselves the originating source of wisdom as we re-construct ourselves?

Moreover, different 'selves' will have interests which conflict with each other, and even with biology. Hence, some prominent persons seem to be unclear what a woman *is*, ontologically. However, others are sufficiently confident in their constructions to give biological males access to women's spaces, sports and other areas which conflict with women's legitimate concerns.[168]

---

[167] We should not take this 'self' to be an isolated or wholly autonomous entity. Carl Trueman notes the influence of other 'selves' within the culture where these selves reside. (Trueman 2020, 73). Hence a 'self' will be influenced by the surrounding ethos. That ethos may give the self a measure of apparent sovereignty, which nevertheless remains constrained by the external cultural ethos.

[168] This topic is not the theme of this book, so I take it no further beyond some examples showing the creative ability of language. For details, see Carl Trueman in the aptly named *The Rise and Triumph of the Modern Self* (2020). In the case of children, an example would be the practices at the Gender Identity Development Service (GIDS) of the Tavistock and Portman NHS Foundation Trust. (Barnes 2023; see also Cass 2024) While the comments in the main text are brief, they are based on such current trends.

Again, we face the question whether this is a manifestation of that tree's fruit, the results of wisdom having its origin in ourselves rather than with God.

But the dilemma can go the other way, particularly for believers. The possibility that our understanding is in some way linguistically 'constructed' by ourselves becomes seriously objectionable, particularly with contemporary trends in mind.

It also becomes objectionable when any material aspects of a Genesis cosmology are apparently mistaken because they are the constructs of an ancient and very different culture. Indeed, the whole edifice of religious and metaphysical beliefs might be nothing more than human constructs. Any notion of an ultimate 'truth' about significance and value seems lost.

Hence, there is a reaction against the term 'construct' and its implications. The alternative to such constructs is that the world and its significance is what it is because that is how God made it; the world is a ready-made given to us.

Our business is then to think God's thoughts after him, as the saying goes. This approach hopes to turn away from us constructing our own understanding of creation and instead to locate the source of wisdom with God Himself, which includes following what is taken to be the clear meaning of scripture.

The intention here is admirable and expresses an important truth, namely, that whatever the nature of this world and its subtle complexity, God made it, including ourselves. However, we may lose sight of our role as rulers or vice-regents.

One reason for this, which is the theme of this book, is that we are detached from the ANE context of the Genesis creation account and its functional ontology of existence. That ontology includes the linguistic aspect of our own role in giving a name, following the archetypal Adam.

Our naming thereby mirrors God's naming, giving us a derivative creativity as we labour to understand God's creation so that we can rule. I characterised this as a 'constructive linguistic' ability. If we eliminate the constructive aspect, we lose something of the theological background to the image of God and our cultural mandate.

In dealing with this dilemma, I have used Adam as the illustrative focus by asking what he was doing in naming the animals in his archetypal role. I then tried to reconcile the dilemma through the image of God and our cultural mandate to rule as God's vice-regents.

To carry out that mandate, I have recognised the creative power of language which mirrors in a secondary and derivative way the creative speaking of God. That was one side of the dilemma.

On the other side, I placed Adam's naming within God's ordered creation and the context of the ANE; this naming is not arbitrary but must take account of that order. And so, we are equipped to continue God's creative work by understanding and producing further order in His creation.

This creative-constructive aspect of our humanity should not be lost in a reaction against contemporary trends, since it manifests the image of God in ourselves, along with our human dignity.

However, there are two important qualifications which result from the image and our cultural mandate. Firstly, God honours and His revelation accommodates, not the evils of individuals and cultures, but cultural differences and perspectives. Furthermore, He does not spoon-feed us to overcome our ignorance on matters within our mandate to rule, such as the development of scientific knowledge.

It is our responsibility to learn about that domain and overcome our ignorance, so that we can then increase the order God has already created.

If ancient peoples and many later ones were mistaken on cosmology and astronomy, it is our business to correct what was mistaken. We will be amazed at what we find and should come to worship the Creator even more profoundly. We are then enabled to create that further order in our own cultural, scientific and artistic developments towards a 'final good'.

But secondly and importantly, our understanding of God Himself is not within Adam's domain to rule, and must be governed by the scriptures. Similarly for the wisdom we need to appreciate significance, value and how to apply these to the goals and ends which we implement in further ordering God's world as His vice-regents.

It is also the significance and dignity of ourselves as human beings that is determined by scripture. That is where we find God's creation purpose for men and women, our being in the image of God and the principles to guide our lives. These are for us to apply but not to construct.

It may be too much to say the dilemma is overcome in a tidy resolution. Nevertheless, this approach does justice to the major considerations, even if a tension remains. It fully affirms our human dignity, the image of God in its linguistic-creative aspect and the mandate which we have been given. On the other hand, the above approach also does justice to scripture and the Genesis creation account placing us within the constraints of an ordered creation.

For my conclusion, I have chosen this dilemma because questions will arise with individuals and churches on these topics. While tensions may remain, they should drive us to consider all aspects of the wider picture. Doing so will give a more unified view, as I have tried to do.

Moreover, we should accept that we will not have all our questions and concerns about God's ways in creation answered. But then, neither did Job as God spoke to him at the end of his suffering: "Where were you when I laid the earth's foundation? Tell me, if you understand." (Job 38:4)

9.2 Contemporary Relevance

Despite all the above, it may be that the reader is not convinced about the creative-constructive character of language and that my development of Adam naming the animals is over-imaginative. Whatever the ANE and Genesis perspective on existence (separation, function, name, order), it is too much to suppose Adam's or our naming brings any kind of further existence into the natural world.

However, when we turn to contemporary trends in many Western societies, the creative use of language is remarkable. What might our linguistic theme have to say about those trends? Does our theme have any relevance beyond that ancient world?

Perhaps any still sceptical readers might yet be persuaded.

Turning first to the creative power of the name, this is readily apparent. Readers need only imagine some of the applications of 'phobia', 'phobic', 'bigot', 'prejudice', 'discrimination' being applied to themselves; the effect can be devastating. It matters little how a person sees themselves; these names are determinative for those who wield them and many who hear them.

Other creative words/names appropriated as advocates for justice and freedom are 'inclusive', 'diverse' and 'affirming'. Some have experienced the reality of such terms as very different from what one might at first suppose. The virtue sense of these functionally descriptive names persists while being appropriated for rather different ends.

Other terms like 'gender-fluid', 'trans-man or woman' and 'non-binary' are remarkable constructed names which, at least for some, convey a reality of self-identity. Such names even trump biology as an identity marker and override the legitimate concerns of women, as I noted earlier.

I am inclined to say that these few examples alone are better illustrations of creative linguistic constructs than any of the examples I have mentioned in earlier chapters.

As for believers, the theme of this book strongly suggests that they take the creative power of the name and other linguistic constructs seriously. Following Adam in his archetypal role, so now nothing less than a new humanity is being constructed.

Is this a consequence as the image of God, which has eaten the fruit from that tree of knowledge, placing ourselves as the origin and source of wisdom? And is all this for good or evil? The question is of the utmost importance, most of all when it affects children and schools.

Since we have a mandate to rule, such a rule will also originate from ourselves as the source of justice. Then, will good and evil be patterned after God's ordering, or be disordered by us? New norms will be and are being enforced by the threat of reputational, employment and financial ruin for dissenting voices.

While supposed patriarchal and other forms of oppressive power are being swept aside, ironically, these are replaced by another set of powers, which may be even more oppressive in their own way.[169]

Moving on from the creative power of the name, do the material and functional ontologies we previously considered have any relevance?

We have seen that a material ontology alone cannot sustain the values to which believers and many others are committed. No science will tell us whether the universe has any meaning and hence, whether human beings have any value, significance or dignity beyond their beliefs.

Furthermore, a self-identifying person is hardly likely to accept a material ontology which might prioritise a material biology. Their commitment is presumably to the sovereign self, which indicates a commitment to a belief and value system closer to a functional than a material ontology. The self now determines and then functions in line with its own sense of self-identity.

Nevertheless, that material ontology remains influential given the background of our current society and its scientific developments. For example,

[169] Carl Trueman notes the way language is changed in his extensive analysis of the modern self under pressure from a new political consensus. (Trueman 2020, 21)

this ontology is apparent in medical practices which work with our biology and genetics.

A person who needs medical treatment will expect that treatment to align with biology where that is relevant to the person's condition, regardless of the way they self-identify. The scientific tradition continues to assert the influence of our material constitution and our dependence on scientific integrity.[170] That is hardly surprising given God as the Creator of the material world.

Let's next consider contemporary trends as a functional ontology. Of course, for secular persons, any contemporary functional purpose is not a transcendent one in accord with the intentions of any gods, or of God, as was the case in the ANE and the Genesis account.

Yet, even if the old divinities are gone, new ones will arrive. *We* now determine our own functioning which includes giving a name, as did those gods of old. For some, choosing or changing a personal name and its pronouns are integral to the person's function.

Such names are chosen to match the gender identity determined not by the gods or by God, but by the self. Where we seek to change the human condition and the organisation of society, it shows a teleological-purposeful direction which is characteristic of a functional ontology in the ANE scheme of existence, including assigning a name.

Hence, a functional ontology is also at work, though unlike the ANE, the ontology is determined by ourselves instead of any divinity, as one would expect from eating the fruit of that tree of knowledge.

Next, we might ask whether there is a place for separation and coming into existence to complete that ANE functional ontology, but now in contemporary

---

[170] In this contentious area we even need to exercise caution around scientific integrity. For example, *Living in Love and Faith* (LLF) is a Church of England programme which considers questions of human sexuality. It fairly presents differing points of view. LLF quotes research, but also warns of the difficulties of conducting such research, and of political bias. For example, Chapter 6 on *Science* contains a number of warnings. (LLF 2020, 105–106; 109; 116)

The conflict between facts, evidence and ideology is striking in the Cass report into medical practices at the Tavistock Gender Identity Development Service. It seems that ideology trumped facts and evidence in supposedly science based medical practices. (Cass 2024)

terms. And surely there is. A new, or various new self-identities, are *separated* from the previous binary and heteronormative identities.

Their function is named to convey the reality of a different kind of existence within the human race. Hence, there is further variety introduced into God's creation by ourselves. Here finally, the image of God is in full bloom. But is this an increase in order or an increasing disorder brought about by eating the fruit from the tree of the knowledge of good and evil?

Coming to a close by returning to what is 'good', we can ask if the functions of self-identification and varied sexualities are also moving towards human flourishing, a *final good*? We are certainly dealing with human relations and ethical questions, which concern the *relational and ethical good.*

That some suppose these are functionally achievable goods is clear enough, hence we have a *functional good.* These various applications of the term 'good' are also further examples of our constructive and creative use of language. While this mirrors in our language the sense of 'good' which we encounter in the Genesis creation account, whose wisdom will determine what is good and evil?

That we creatively construct various linguistic 'goods' is apparent, but that does not make them good. For any *final good*, our constructing must seek God's order in creation by His wisdom rather than our own. We are now left with the question: what is the 'good' in the above controversies?

Perhaps disappointingly for some, that question goes beyond the scope of this book, which is a scriptural view of the constructive and creative use of language. Neither are we concerned with the very important matter of pastoral responses to those who are questioning their identity, and in some cases distressed.

Certainly no one is to be rejected by believers or the church. All of us are affected by that fruit of the tree of knowledge in different ways and degrees; no one is any better than anyone else. From a Christian or creation worldview which I have tried to maintain, any good will need to be based on both scripture and an ethos of mutual support and love within the church.

So, we finish with perhaps the most important point of relevance, which is that other tree, the tree of life. We may indeed acquire a new name and identity, though these are not of our own making. Neither will they be given us by anyone who has eaten the fruit from that tree of knowledge.

Our new name and identity will be given us by Jesus Christ along with a new birth and life, and thereby the promise of the tree of life will be realised. That promise will embody an eternal and divine-functional purpose or final good in a new created order. There we will abide with God, not in a temple building but in the renewed cosmic temple of creation. All that is even now available to us:

> "The one who is victorious I will make a pillar in the temple of my God. Never again will they leave it. I will write on them the name of my God and the name of the city of my God, the new Jerusalem, which is coming down out of heaven from my God; and I will also write on them my new name."
>
> (Rev. 3:12)

Glossary

The descriptions which follow are brief and broad-brush summaries of terms set in a varied background of complex human practices and belief systems. Boundaries are not tidy, and in some cases the use of these terms are closely inter-related, again without a neat demarcation.

Archetype: An archetype embodies all individuals in a group where the group shares characteristics of the archetype. An archetype may be an actual individual but the emphasis is less on the individual than on the overarching truth or symbolic value of the originating archetype which applies to those who follow in the archetype's characteristics.

The concept of the 'archetype' is used in other areas of literature and art where it is a recurrent symbol or motif, and in Jungian psychology. Perhaps Romeo and Juliet are themselves literary archetypes which still evoke strong human emotions.

The use of typology terms in scripture or further developed by ourselves is varied. For example, Adam is "a type of the one to come." (Rom. 5:14) Christ is then referred to as the 'antitype'. We are not concerned with variants in typology terms and have simply referred to Adam as an 'archetype', a ruling or original type for those who follow.

Construct: In the context of human ideas and beliefs, a 'construct' is an idea, belief or theory generated by ourselves to explain or describe something of interest or concern to us.

There is a creative aspect to our constructs where something of our personality and background enters our judgements and thereby the way we perceive or understand. With the examples in this book, I emphasise that constructs need to work with the experienced realities of human life and the world in which we find ourselves. Even so, a wholly objective, person or culture-independent perspective is not possible.

***Cosmos*:** This term is interchangeable with 'universe' or 'creation'. The original ancient Greek understanding also had the sense of an orderly world. That sense of order would apply to the ancient Near East (ANE) and also to much of our modern scientific knowledge.

***Culture*:** This term refers to the ideas, beliefs and practices of a particular society. The term 'culture' does not merely refer to a particular social group but to their shared beliefs and practices.

***Empiricism*:** A philosophical position which holds that knowledge is based on experience through our senses, along with logical relations that hold within experience. Logical relations may be true by definition: 'All bachelors are unmarried men'. Logical relations may also apply to evidence: "The accused cannot be in London and Paris at the same time."

Empiricism does justice to everyday experience where we can often, or at least in principle, determine whether something is true of false beyond being a matter of belief or opinion. It also gives a place to scientific knowledge based on testing and evidence.

However, empiricism as a philosophical principle cannot be derived from experience and so cannot be known to be true by its own premise.

Since judgements of value, human significance and many religious beliefs are not matters of experience and cannot be derived from the facts which we can investigate, they are thereby not knowledge in the empiricist sense. They are likely to be relegated to sentiments and beliefs.

Ex-nihilo: In the context of creation, ex-nihilo is to create from nothing, on the assumption that there was no previous material or anything else to create something from.

Creation ex-nihilo is not merely a re-shaping or re-forming of already existent matter. There is philosophical principle that 'nothing comes from nothing', which then takes ex-nihilo to imply a creation by a creative power which exists eternally to or outside of what is created.

Function: In respect to the ANE, the terms 'function' and 'functional ontology' refer to that ancient predominant concern with the purpose or ends of aspects of creation in relation to the gods and the maintenance of order. This is to use a contemporary technical term and apply it to the ancient context, which we should not distort in using the term.

Our contemporary use of 'function' is a material-causal term which in some cases also has a teleological sense. Good examples are our artefacts and the biological sciences. Our contemporary teleological sense has helpful similarities to the ANE creation accounts but any material-causal aspect of a function was of little interest in ANE creation stories, including the Genesis account.

See also Ontology—Functional.

Ideology: A way of looking at the organisation and political/social/historical processes in societies, often through the perspective of a theory or idea which becomes an overriding logos or principle of reason. The underlying idea may be based on a truth about specific social injustices, which then pushes aside other perspectives. Contrary arguments and evidence are subordinated to the ideology.

An ideology often has a significant emphasis on achieving social change. Being a logos of reason and often also of social righteousness, there is a tendency to suppress opposition and itself become oppressive. Hence, ideologies often to not seek just to explain but to change social systems and practices.

An ideology is similar to a worldview and a related metanarrative, though the focus of an ideology is narrower than that of a worldview, as is implicit in the terms themselves.

Literal: We generally take this to mean as experienced through the senses, matters of fact or what is verifiable in experience and everyday familiar life. There is no metaphor or exaggeration involved. For example, to say, "I am starving," is generally not taken to mean in a poor physical condition due to lack of food, which is the literal sense of 'starving'.

The use of 'starving' here is exaggerated whereas the literal equivalent is 'very hungry' and rather humdrum.

Matter/Material-cause-process-structure: By 'matter' and 'material', we refer to all the complex variety of 'stuff' that makes up the universe, including our own bodies. We encounter matter as material structures and cause-effect processes. We might also speak of corporeal bodies or substances having mass, dimensions and spatial locations which behave according to laws of physics.

This material corporeal world becomes somewhat less corporeal as we understand something of its underlying particle and quantum structure from the physical sciences.

The corporeal-material also has a more ambiguous relation if we contrast *mind* with the matter of the brain, or contrast the concrete character of the material structures and processes with the abstract character of the mathematics which describes them.

See also Ontology—Material.

***Metanarrative*:** An overarching story or set of ideas which give a group or society their self-understanding and place in the world. The Genesis creation account would be such a metanarrative, as are the creation myths of the ANE and elsewhere around the world. A metanarrative is related to a worldview and somewhat less closely to an ideology.

***Metaphysics*:** A branch of philosophy which deals with the nature of reality. 'Reality' is itself a questionable and vague term, but then metaphysics should bring some clarity.

However, the subject is varied and disputed. For our purposes, a metaphysical approach is to explain how our experience through the senses, or what is concluded from scientific investigations and the understanding of the mind, mirrors or in some way accurately conveys to us how things are in themselves apart from our faculties.

In other words, whether things as they appear to us, or are theorised or judged by us, accurately represents the 'reality'. Metaphysical questions underlie knowledge (epistemology), ethics, aesthetics and many other subjects.

***Ontology*:** This is the study of the existence of something, and what it is to be one thing rather than another. Ontological questions are another motivation for philosophical theories concerned with the existence or being of specific things, and particularly with the existence and being in general as it might apply to all existent things. Ontology is closely connected with how we can know such matters, which is *epistemology*.

Ontology—Functional: The term 'functional ontology' is used in this book for the dominant perspective of the ANE where the business of the gods is to maintain order within the cosmos. That order is functional in that the elements of the cosmos, including the gods, have their role within the overall order.

The 'ontological' aspect is how the components of the cosmos, in being what they are, contribute to the overall order.

Ontology—Material: A 'material ontology' is the dominant contemporary perspective, though not necessarily in all cultures. It is significantly shaped by scientific developments and deals with what something is from a material aspect.

***Paradigm*:** We used the term in connection with the physical sciences. Here, a paradigm is the prevailing scientific consensus on theories and the current state of scientific knowledge.

Paradigms might we described as the current prevailing 'normal science' which supplies the tools and problems on which scientists work and which are applied in fundamental research, engineering, medicine and much else. Anomalies may lead to a paradigm shift where the new paradigm is in some ways incompatible with the previous paradigm.

Real, Reality: The sum total of everything which actually exists. Reality might be distinguished from what is only imagined and does not actually exist. This definition is rather vague and dependent on what we mean by 'exist' and further complicated by what we 'know' to exist.

Hence, when we use the term 'real' or 'reality', there are likely to be philosophical objections about what we mean by the term and that it is far too vague to be of much use.

***Relativism*:** This is a philosophical position which claims that beliefs about values, significance and other ultimate truths about the world and ourselves are dependent on the cultures which hold them. Such beliefs differ and may have come about by historical, economic, environmental, evolutionary or any number of circumstances.

Hence, the resultant beliefs do not reflect anything beyond those circumstance and the cultures which hold them. These beliefs are 'relative' to the culture, and that is the case with all such beliefs about ultimate significance, truth and 'reality'.

Syntax/Semantics: 'Syntax' refers to the order and the rules of grammar in a sentence or language. 'Semantics' refers to the meaning thereby conveyed. In using these terms, we need to remember that semantics is not entirely a question of grammar and rules, but also how these are woven into human life and practices. Talk about syntax and semantics is liable to lose sight of human practices.

***Taxonomy*:** In general terms, taxonomy is the science of classification applied in a variety of disciplines. The example in this book is with biological taxonomy, which is a hierarchical system of classification of living systems. The first modern biological taxonomy was devised by Carl Linnaeus in 1753.

***Teleology*:** The way something is directed towards a goal, end or has a purpose. 'Teleology' is often a broadest category for something being goal-directed with other terms also being 'teleological'. For example, the following can have a teleological sense: end, goal, purpose, intention, role, function.

***Worldview*:** A wide-ranging perspective on the world and human life which addresses questions of human significance, ultimate purpose and value. Such questions might include 'Why are we here?' and 'Is there any purpose to human life and the material universe?' Religions address such questions but so does atheism or materialism.

While some aspects of a worldview are clearly stated, other aspects may be hidden and thereby presupposed. A worldview, including its hidden assumptions, will influence judgements which are supposed to evaluate arguments. The resulting conclusions may then reflect and confirm the worldview.

A worldview is similar to a metanarrative with some similarities to an ideology, where the worldview is more wide-ranging, as is implicit in the term itself.

Bibliography

Al-Khalili, Jim and McFadden, Johnjoe. (2014) *Life on the Edge: The Coming of Age of Quantum Biology*, London: Bantam Press.

Allen, C., Bekoff, M. and Lauder, G. (eds.) (1998) *Nature's Purposes: Analysis of Function and Design in Biology*, London: The MIT Press.

Allen, Colin and Neal, Jacob. (2020) *'Teleological Notions in Biology'*, The Stanford Encyclopaedia of Philosophy (Spring 2020 Edition), Edward N. Zalta (ed.) Available from:
<https://plato.stanford.edu/archives/spr2020/entries/teleology-biology/>
[Accessed 21 August 2023]

Alexander, Denis. (2014) *Creation or Evolution—Do we need to choose?* (2nd Edition), Oxford: Monarch Books.

Alexander, Denis. (2018) *Is there Purpose in Biology?* Oxford: Lion Hudson Limited.

Andersen, M. L. and Hill Collins, P. (1995) *Race, Class and Gender—An Anthology* (2nd Edition), Wadsworth Publishing Company.

Aristotle, (1938) *VOL. 1, On Interpretation*. Loeb Classical Library Volume 325. H.P.Cooke & Hugh Tredennick (trans). Cambridge, Massachusetts: Harvard University Press.

Aristotle. (1976) *Aristotle-Ethics,* J. A. K. Thomson (trans), London: Penguin Books.

Aristotle. (1998) *The Metaphysics,* H. Lawson-Tancred (trans), London: Penguin Books.

Aristotle. (1999) *Physics,* R. Waterfield (trans), Oxford: Oxford University Press.

Aristotle. (2004) *On the Parts of Animals,* James G. Lennox (trans), Oxford: Clarendon Press. Available from:

<https://library.uoh.edu.iq/admin/ebooks/37569-aristotle_on_the_parts_of_animals_i-iv_compressed.pdf> [Accessed 21 August 2023]

Aristotle. (2005) *The Ethics of Aristotle*, Project Gutemberg. Available from: <https://www.gutenberg.org/cache/epub/8438/pg8438-images.html#chap01> [Accessed 21 December 2023]

Augustine. (1955) *Augustine: Confessions*, Albert C. Outler (ed and trans). Georgetown University. Available from: <https://faculty.georgetown.edu/jod/augustine/conf.pdf> [Accessed 23 December 2023]

Ayer, A. J. (1936) *Language, Truth and Logic*, London: Penguin Books.

Baghramian, Maria and J. Adam Carter. (2022) *'Relativism'*, The Stanford Encyclopaedia of Philosophy (Spring 2022 Edition), Edward N. Zalta (ed.) Available from: <https://plato.stanford.edu/archives/spr2022/entries/relativism/> [Accessed 5 September 2023]

Barnes, Hannah. (2023) *Time to Think—The Inside Story of the Collapse of the Tavistock's Gender Services for Children,* London: Swift Press.

Bellos, Alex. (2010) *Alex's Adventures in Numberland*, London: Bloomsbury.

Biggar, Nigel. (2023) *Colonialism—A Moral Reckoning*, London: Harper Colling Publishers.

Bird, A. (2003) *Philosophy of Science*, London: Routledge.

Bird, Alexander. (2002) *'Thomas Kuhn'*, The Stanford Encyclopaedia of Philosophy (Spring 2022 Edition), Edward N. Zalta (ed.) Available from: <https://plato.stanford.edu/archives/spr2022/entries/thomas-kuhn/> [Accessed 21 August 2023]

Cass, Hilary, (2024) *The Cass Review*, Available from: <https://cass.independent-review.uk/home/publications/final-report/> [Accessed 8 June 2024]

Church of England, (2020) *Living in Love and Faith*, London: Church House Publishing.

Cohan, S. and Shires, L. M. (1997) *Telling Stories—A Theoretical Analysis of Narrative Fiction*, London and New York: Routledge.

Dalley, Stephanie, (2008) *Myths from Mesopotamia—Creation, The Flood, Gilgamesh and Others*. Oxford: Oxford University Press.

Davies, P. (2006) *The Goldilocks Enigma*, London: Penguin Books.

Derrida, Jacques. (1976) *Of Grammatology*, Baltimore and London: The Johns Hopkins University Press.

Descartes, R. (1968) *Discourse on Method and the Meditations*, London: Penguin Books.

Dirckx, Sharon. (2019) *Am I just my brain?* The Good Book Company.

Falcon, Andrea. (2023) *'Aristotle on Causality'*, The Stanford Encyclopaedia of Philosophy (Spring 2023 Edition), Edward N. Zalta and Uri Nodelman (eds.) Available from: <https://plato.stanford.edu/archives/spr2023/entries/aristotle-causality/> [Accessed 21 August 2023]

Flew, A. with Varghese, R. A. (2007) *There is a God*, New York: Harper One.

Frahm, Eckart. (2023) *Assyria—The Rise and Fall of the World's First Empire*, London: Bloomsbury Publishing.

Frankfurt, H. G. (1964) *'The Logic of Omnipotence'*, The Philosophical Review, **73**, 2, 262–263.

Gaukroger, Stephen. (2008) *The Emergence of a Scientific Culture, Science and the Shaping of Modernity 1210-1685,* Oxford: Clarendon Press.

Hardin, Jeff. (2019). *Biology and Theological Anthropology: Friends or Foes?* Available from:
<https://cms.biologos.org/wp-content/uploads/2019/12/Biology-and-Theological-Anthropology-Friends-or-Foes.pdf> [Accessed on25 March 2024]

Hilber, John, W. (2020) *Old Testament Cosmology and Divine Accommodation*, Eugene, Oregon: Cascade Books.

Hippocrates. (1989) *Loeb Classical Library: Hippocrates Vol II-The Sacred Disease*, W. H. S Jones (trans), Cambridge, Massachusetts and London: Harvard University Press.

Holdcroft, D. (1991) *Saussure: Signs, System and Arbitrariness*, Cambridge: Cambridge University Press.

Hooykaas, R. (1973) *Religion and the Rise of Modern Science*, Edinburgh and London: Scottish Academic.

Horowitz, Wayne. (2011) *Mesopotamian Cosmic Geo*graphy, Winona Lake, Indiana: Eisenbrauns.
Hume, D. (1985) *A Treatise of Human Nature*, London: Penguin Books.
Hume, D. (1999) *An Enquiry concerning Human Understanding*, Oxford: Oxford University Press.
Hurowitz, Victor. (1992) *I have built you an exalted house*, Sheffield: Sheffield Academic Press.

James, Sharon. (2021) *How Christianity transformed the World*, Glasgow: Christian Focus.

Kant, Immanuel, (1996), *Critique of Pure Reasons*. London: Everyman.
Keil, C. F. and Delitzsch, F. (1975) *Commentary on the Old Testament, Volume 1, The Pentateuch*, James Martin, (trans), Grand Rapids, Michigan: William B. Eerdmans Publishing Company.
Kraut, Richard. (2022) *Aristotle's Ethics*, The Stanford Encyclopaedia of Philosophy (Fall 2022 Edition), Edward N. Zalta and Uri Nodelman (eds.) Available from: <https://plato.stanford.edu/archives/fall2022/entries/aristotle-ethics/> [Accessed 21 August 2023]
Kuhn, T. S. (1970) *The Structure of Scientific Revolutions* (2nd Edition), Chicago: University of Chicago Press.

Lakoff, G. (2004) *Ten Lectures on Cognitive Linguistics—Lecture 8*. YouTube: <www.youtube.com/watch?v=8CUkZc7sLXE> [Accessed 4 May 2023]
Linnebo, Øystein. (2023) *'Platonism in the Philosophy of Mathematics'*, The Stanford Encyclopaedia of Philosophy (Summer 2023 Edition), Edward N. Zalta and Uri Nodelman (eds.) Available from:
<https://plato.stanford.edu/archives/sum2023/entries/platonism-mathematics/> [Accessed 30 August 2023].
Lipton, P. (2004) *Inference to the Best Explanation* (2nd Edition), London and New York: Routledge.
Longman III, Tremper and Walton, John, H. (2018) *The Lost World of the Flood*, Downers Grove, Illinois: IVP Academic.
Lyotard, Jean-François. (1997) *The Postmodern Condition: A Report on Knowledge*, Manchester: Manchester University Press.

Madueme, Hans and Reeves, Michael (eds.) (2014) *Adam, the Fall, and Original Sin—Theological, Biblical and Scientific Perspectives*, Grand Rapids, Michigan: Baker Academic.

Mark, J. (2018) *'Enuma Elish—The Babylonian Epic of Creation—Full Text'*, World History Encyclopaedia. Available from: www.worldhistory.org. [Accessed 21 August 2023]

Mavrodes, George, I. (2007) *'Some Puzzles Concerning Omnipotence'*, Philosophy of Religion—Selected Readings (3rd Edition), New York and Oxford: Oxford University Press.

McGrath, Alister E. (2009) *A Fine-Tuned Universe*. Louisville, Kentucky: Westminster John Knox Press.

McMullin, Ernan, (2019) *The Galileo Affair*. Has Science Killed God, The Faraday Papers on Science and Religion. D.Alexander (ed). London: The Faraday Institute, SPCK.

Moore, G. (1996) *Believing in God—A Philosophical Essay*, Edinburgh: T&T Clark Ltd.

Moyal-Sharrock, D. (2007) *Understanding Wittgenstein's 'On Certainty'*, Basingstoke: Palgrave Macmillan.

Nagel, Ernest, and Newman, James R. (1981), *Gödel's Proof*. London: Routledge and Keegan Paul Ltd.

Newton-Smith, W. H. (1996) *The Rationality of Science*, London and New York: Routledge.

Øhrstrøm, Peter and Hasle, Per. (2020) *Future Contingents*, The Stanford Encyclopedia of Philosophy (Summer 2020 Edition), Edward N. Zalta (ed.), URL = <https://plato.stanford.edu/archives/sum2020/entries/future-contingents> [Accessed 20 February 2022]

Paul, Ian. (2018) *Revelation-Tyndale New Testament Commentaries*, London: IVP Academic.

Phillips, D. Z. (1993) *Wittgenstein and Religion,* London: The Macmillan Press.

Plato. (1977) *Timaeus and Critias*, D. Lee (trans), London: Penguin Books.

Plato. (2013) *Euthyphro*. B. Jowett (trans), 'Project Gutenberg'. Available from: <www.gutenberg.org>

Plato. (2021) *'Euthydemus'*, David Horan (trans), Foundation for Platonic Studies. Available from:
<Euthydemus-The Dialogues of Plato (platonicfoundation.org)> [Accessed 27 September 2023]

Popper, K. (1980) *Unended Quest*, Glasgow: Fontana/Collins.

Polanyi, M. (1974) *Personal Knowledge*, Chicago: University of Chicago Press.

Potter, Jonathan. (1997) *Representing Reality—Discourse, Rhetoric and Social Construction*, London: SAGE Publications Ltd.

Rhees, R. (2004) *In Dialogue with the Greeks, Volume 1—The Presocratics and Reality*, D. Z. Phillips (ed.) Aldershot: Ashgate Publishing Limited.

De Saussure, F. (1966) *Course in General Linguistics*, C. Bally and A. Sechehaye (eds.) W. Baskin (trans), New York: McGraw-Hill.

Shakespeare (n.d.) *'Romeo and Juliet from The Folger Shakespeare'*, Barbara Mowat, Paul Werstine, Michael Poston, Rebecca Niles (eds.) Folger Shakespeare Library. Available from: <https://folger.edu/explore/shakespeares-works/romeo-and-juliet/> [Accessed 21 August 2023]

Singer, I. B. (1980) *A Friend of Kafka and other stories*, Harmondsworth: Penguin Books.

Smith Churchland, Patricia. (2002) *Brain-Wise, Studies in Neuro philosophy*, Cambridge, Massachusetts: A Bradford Book, The MIT Press.

Spencer, Nick. (2016) *The Evolution of the West*, London: SPCK.

Swinburne, R. (2004) *The Existence of God* (2nd Edition), Oxford: Clarendon Press.

Trueman, Carl, R. (2020) *The Rise and Triumph of the Modern Self*, Wheaton, Illinois: Crossway.

Walton, John, H. (2009) *The Lost World of Genesis One*, Illinois: IVP Academic.

Walton, John, H. (2015a) *Genesis 1 as Ancient Cosmology*, Indiana: Eigenbranes.

Walton, John, H. (2015b) *The Lost World of Adam and Eve*, Illinois: IVP Academic.

Walton, John, H. (2018) *Ancient Near Eastern Thought and the Old Testament*, Grand Rapids, Michigan: Baker Academic.

Webster, C. W. (1975) *The Great Instauration: Science, Medicine, Reform*, 1626–1660. London: Duckworth.

Wenham, Gordon, J. (1987) *'Word Biblical Commentary'*, Nelson Reference and Electronic, 1, Genesis 1–5.

Wigner, Eugene. (1960) *'The Unreasonable Effectiveness of Mathematics in the Natural Sciences'*, Communications in Pure and Applied Mathematics, 13, I (February 1960). New York: John Wiley & Sons.
Available from: <https://www.maths.ed.ac.uk/~v1ranick/papers/wigner.pdf> [Accessed 1 October 2023]

Wittgenstein, L. (1974) *Tractatus Logico-Philosophicus*, D. F. Pears and B. F. McGuiness (trans), London and New York: Routledge.

Wittgenstein, L. (1997) *Philosophical Investigations* (2nd edit.), G. E. M. Anscombe (trans), Oxford: Blackwell.

Wittgenstein, L. (2006) *On Certainty,* D. Paul and G. E. M. Anscombe (trans), Oxford: Blackwell Publishing.

Wright, L. (1976) *Teleological Explanations*, London: University of California Press.

Zalasiewicz, J. and Williams, M. (2012) *The Goldilocks Planet,* Oxford: Oxford University Press.

Scripture and other Acknowledgements

Scripture quotations taken from:
The Holy Bible, New International Version (Anglicised edition)
Copyright © 1979, 1984, 2011 by Biblica (formerly International Bible Society). Used by permission of Hodder & Stoughton Publishers, an Hachette UK company. All rights reserved.
'NIV' is a registered trademark of Biblica (formerly International Bible Society). UK trademark number 1448790

ARISTOTLE, VOL. I, translated by H. P. Cooke and Hugh Tredennick, Loeb Classical Library Volume 325, Cambridge, Mass.: Harvard University Press, 1938.
Loeb Classical Library ® is a registered trademark of the President and Fellows of Harvard College. Used by permission. All rights reserved.

WORD BIBLICAL COMMENTARY, VOLUME 1, GENESIS 1–5 by Gordon J. Wenham. Copyright © 1987 by Word, Incorporated. Used by permission of HarperCollins Christian Publishing. www.harpercollinschristian.com

TELLING STORIES—A THEORETICAL ANALYSIS OF NARRATIVE FICTION by Cohan, S. and Shires, L.M., Copyright © 1988 Steven Cohan and Linda M. Shires. Reproduced with permission of the Licensor, INFORMA UK LTD through PLSclear.

MYTHS FROM MESOPOTAMIA—CREATION, THE FLOOD, GILGAMESH AND OTHERS, A new translation by Stephanie Dalley, Copyright © 1989 Stephanie Dalley. Reproduced with permission of the Licensor, Oxford Publishing Ltd through PLSclear.

THE POSTMODERN CONDITION: A REPORT ON KNOWLEDGE by Jean-François Lyotard, Copyright © 1979 by Les Editions de Minuit. Reproduced with permission of the Licensor, The University of Manchester through PLSclear.

Index